# Stop My Crisis

# Facing Life's Challenges Head-On

By

Vivian C. Gaspar

The content within this book is not intended to take the place of a consultation with a qualified professional regarding the reader's specific circumstances.

This book's ISBN categories are:
Finance, Business, Self-Help Technique

Published by:
Carpe 28, LLC
Succasunna, NJ

2015 Copyright Pending

No part of this book may be reproduced without written consent.

Copyright © 2015 Carpe 28, LLC

All rights reserved.

ISBN: 978-0-9832-121-2-6    51982

# Dedication

This book, and all my dreams of helping as many people as possible through education on a broad variety of topics, is due to my love for the people closest to me. My mother had always dreamed I would become a writer by profession (specifically a journalist), since I had started writing short stories and poems when I was very young. (I was accepted into the Accelerated Creative Writing Program at Montclair State University when I was 15.) I actually had always attributed my entrepreneurial spirit to my father, who had always been an inspiration as I saw him try his hand at many businesses ever since I was young and throughout my adulthood. Therefore, I am quite happy to say that this book, to be the first in a series, can be attributed to both my parents, whom I love deeply.

I would also like to dedicate this book to Richard Frantz, who has been the single most influential individual in my adult life and has always been very supportive of my entrepreneurial endeavors, including this book series.

Also, I am also very appreciative and grateful to have worked with V. James Castiglia in the mortgage modification arena. I not only appreciate Jim Castiglia's hard work and dedication to his clients, but I also really enjoyed learning from him in the countless client meetings I had the privilege to witness. Mr. Castiglia's broad knowledge base and his manner of delivering that knowledge in a comforting and tireless fashion is always an inspiration to me; I felt driven in my work because of it. Without Mr. Castiglia and my experiences working for and with him and his exceptional staff, this book would never have been possible. Thank you, Jim!

# Vivian C. Gaspar

# Table of Contents

Dedication .................................................................... iii

Foreword ..................................................................... vii

Acknowledgements ...................................................... ix

**Chapter 1:** Your Credit & How to Improve It, By Peter Nagy ........................................................................................ 10

**Chapter 2:** Identity Theft & Protection, By Vivian C. Gaspar ........................................................................................ 25

**Chapter 3:** Debt Settlement, By Rocco Sileo ..................... 31

**Chapter 4:** Bankruptcy Basics, By Santo Bonanno, Esq. ..... 35

**Chapter 5:** Getting Yourself to College, By Stacey Plichta Kellar, Sc.D. .................................................................... 39

**Chapter 6:** Get Educated for Low to No Cost, By Darsi D. Beauchamp, Ph.D. ........................................................... 47

**Chapter 7:** What is Time Management?, By Arnold Rintzler ........................................................................................ 50

**Chapter 8:** Goal Setting, By Arnold Rintzler ..................... 59

**Chapter 9:** Finding the Right Financial Advisor, By Brian Cody .............................................................................. 68

**Chapter 10:** Financially Surviving Natural Disasters, By Terrence Coughlin, CPCU, ARM, AICA ........................... 71

**Chapter 11:** How a Private Investigator Can Help You Get Money, By Alexander Toia ............................................... 74

**Chapter 12:** Acing Your Next Job Interview, By Joanne Lucas .............................................................................. 79

**Chapter 13:** The Right Answers for Those Tricky Interview Questions, By Joanne Lucas ................................................. 84

**Chapter 14:** How to Get Your Recruiter to Focus on You, By Joanne Lucas .................................................................. 87

**Chapter 15:** Direct Marketing: A Real Income Alternative, By Camille Re ....................................................................... 92

**Chapter 16:** Making Money from Home, By Vivian C. Gaspar ............................................................................................ 98

**Chapter 17:** LinkedIn: The Job Seeker's New Secret Weapon, By Julbert J. Abraham ...................................................... 102

**Chapter 18:** The Real Estate Buying Guide, By Frances Pepe ............................................................................................... 105

**Chapter 19:** Understanding Mortgages, By Stephanie Banks ............................................................................................... 111

**Chapter 20:** Mortgage Modification: Use it to Save Your Home and Sanity, By Vivian C. Gaspar & V. James Castiglia, Esq. ....................................................................................... 129

**Chapter 21:** Understanding the Foreclosure Process, By Vivian C. Gaspar & V. James Castiglia, Esq. ...................... 135

**Chapter 22:** Save On Your Energy Bills, By Michael Menihan ............................................................................................ 139

**Chapter 23:** Should I Pay Off My Mortgage Early?, By Brian Cody ............................................................................................. 142

**Chapter 24:** Reverse Mortgages: A Financial Option for Seniors, By Zoltan Simon, Esq. ............................................. 145

**Chapter 25:** Who knew cleaning toilets could boost self-esteem?, By Fern Weis ............................................................ 152

**Chapter 26:** Get Special Education Help for Students with Disabilities at No Cost, By Darsi D. Beauchamp, Ph.D. ... 154

**Chapter 27:** Are you crippling your kids? Tough love Rx for parents, By Fern Weis ....................................................... 177

**Chapter 28:** It's not your job to make sure your kids are happy, By Fern Weis .......... 180

**Chapter 29:** College Prep Goes On for Years: Taking the Angst Out of the Apps, By Fern Weis .......... 182

**Chapter 30:** What to do When Your Spouse Says: "I'm Outta Here!", By Carolyn N. Daly .......... 186

**Chapter 31:** Divorce Mediation: A Practical Way to Lessen the Costs and Stress, By Robert McDonnell, MS, APM .... 194

**Chapter 32:** I am Not a Victim of Domestic Violence - Speak up & GET OUT!, By Dr. Tamika Anderson .......... 199

**Chapter 33:** Elder Care: Tough Questions for Your Parents, By Tracey S. Lawrence .......... 202

**Chapter 34:** Medicare and Long Term Care: The Middle Class Crisis, By Frank R. Campisano .......... 205

**Chapter 35:** Free At-Home Assistance for Veterans, By Bonnie Laiderman .......... 207

**Chapter 36:** Government Benefits for Low-Income Individuals, By Darsi D. Beauchamp, Ph.D. .......... 208

**Chapter 37:** Understanding Your COBRA Benefits, By Harry Herbst .......... 214

**Chapter 38:** Understanding Obamacare: The Affordable Care Act, By Harry Herbst .......... 216

**Chapter 39:** Medical Care Discount Plans, By Ciro J. Giue .......... 218

**Chapter 40:** Frequently Asked Tax Questions, By Jack M. Bleiberg, CPA .......... 222

**Chapter 41:** I Owe the IRS…Help!, By Jack M. Bleiberg, CPA .......... 227

About the Contributing Authors .......... 231

# Foreword

As someone who has worked individually in the last two years with over 300 families in financial crisis as the Public Relations Director and Mortgage Modification Specialist with the legal office of V. James Castiglia in New Jersey, I found myself hearing similar stories and repeatedly giving the same advice. In addition to assisting couples with the proper completion of mortgage modification applications, I also gave advice on a range of topics where I had developed expertise. My experience includes owning a marketing company, being a recruiter, and helping people decipher their current mortgages; mortgage loan officer and now alternative lending specialist.

One of my responsibilities as Mr. Castiglia's Public Relations Director was to give speeches to civic organizations, such as the Lions Club and Rotary Club, at their locations in New Jersey, as well as the Department of Labor, public libraries, and The Learning Annex. After many of these speeches, during which I would educate the members of these clubs, I was approached to spread my information to a wider audience and to consider writing a book.

In February of 2010, I started to give the idea of writing a book on mortgage modification and the foreclosure process more serious consideration. However, I wanted to have a wider impact. As I gave this idea more thought, I concluded that I could help a wider base of people in crisis if I covered a broad subject base. As I started an outline of chapters and topics I wanted to see included in my book, I immediately thought of all the business contacts I had accumulated over the years. This book is my opportunity to bring to you the knowledge of seasoned professionals on specific topics where they have great expertise.

For many years now I have educated people on topics ranging from "Mortgage Trivia for Everyone" and "Identity Theft and Understanding the Basics of Credit Scores" to "Understanding Mortgage Modification and the Foreclosure Process." Now I want to bring to people the most concisely worded information on a variety of the most critical financial survival topics which everyone can use at one low price.

Please enjoy the journey of learning contained within the following pages, and please e-mail me at Vivian@StopMyCrisis.com telling me how the information in this book has helped to improve your life.

Thank you, and happy reading!

Vivian C. Gaspar

# Acknowledgements

As the creator of this reference book, I would like to take the time to express my gratitude to the 27 professionals without whom this book could never have come to fruition.

First and foremost, I really want to acknowledge and thank my parents. Thanks also to Richard Frantz, my editor and closest companion of the last 26 years, who has been instrumental in my being able to bring this book to its completion; it has been an ongoing challenge to support the time and energy that I needed to devote to this project.

I am extremely grateful to the 27 authors who were very generous with their time and sharing their expertise. I believe that these gracious individuals should be commended for their generosity, since all of them have very busy professional practices.

Another critical member of my team is Jim Castiglia, who is my staff attorney and contributing co-author on several chapters and the reason for this book's very existence.

Vivian C. Gaspar

# Chapter 1

# Your Credit & How to Improve It

## By Peter Nagy

Congratulations! This might seem like a strange thing to say to someone who realizes that they need to "do something" about their credit, whether you know it's not good, you've been avoiding correcting an embarrassing problem on it, or you simply think that there is nothing that can be done to improve it. We all know by now that you need to have good credit for a wide variety of reasons. Some of the reasons that good credit scores are important are well-known; others are not. However, for most of us, how good credit is obtained and how bad credit can be corrected remain a mystery…until now.

Did you realize the ways in which your credit report is judged? BIG NEWS! The three top ways that a credit report is judged, which have nothing to do with being approved for loans, are:

- <u>Being hired</u> – Did you know it is now common practice for hiring companies to judge applicants on their credit reports? They are judging the applicant's character based on the information they see on their credit report. Is that applicant a responsible person with their own finances? If not, does that mean they will not be a good hire? Does outstanding child support show on the credit report? (If so, that person could be judged as a "deadbeat parent.")

-<u>Auto insurance or homeowners insurance/renters insurance</u> – someone can be denied insurance or be charged a surcharge if the credit report deems the person to have irresponsible or high-risk behaviors. So you could have no DMV points on your driver's license, but be charged an auto insurance surcharge simply due to the information on your credit report.

-<u>Renting an apartment or house</u> – we all know that good credit is vital to obtaining a mortgage, but remember that landlords usually look at credit reports when choosing their next tenant. Don't let where you rent be predicated by what is on your credit report.

<u>How FICO® Credit Scores Work When You Apply for Credit</u> – whether for a credit card, a car loan, or a mortgage –lenders want to know what risk they're taking by loaning you money.

FICO® (Fair, Isaac and Company) scores are the credit scores most lenders use to determine your credit risk. You have three FICO® scores, one for each of the three credit bureaus – Experian, TransUnion, and Equifax. Each credit score is based on information the credit bureau keeps on file about you. As this information changes, your credit score tends to change as well.

Your three FICO® credit scores affect both how much money and what loan terms (interest rate, etc.) lenders will offer you at any given time.

1. Payment History 35%
   • Account payment information on specific types of accounts (credit cards, retail accounts, installment loans, finance company accounts, mortgage, etc.)
   • Presence of adverse public records (bankruptcy, judgments, suits, liens, wage attachments, etc.)

- Collection items, and/or delinquency (past due items)
- Severity of delinquency (how long past due)
- Amount past due on delinquent accounts or collection items
- Time since past due items (delinquency), adverse public records (if any), or collection items (if any)
- Number of past due items on file
- Number of accounts paid as agreed

2. Amounts Owed 30%
    - Amount owing on accounts/amount owing on specific types of accounts
    - Lack of a specific type of balance, in some cases
    - Number of accounts with balances
    - Proportion of credit lines used (proportion of balances to total credit limits on certain types of revolving accounts)
    - Proportion of installment loan amounts still owing (proportion of balance to original loan amount on certain types of installment loans)

3. Length of Credit History 15%
    - Time since accounts opened
    - Time since accounts opened, by specific type of account: installment, revolving, monthly
    - Time since account activity

4. New Credit 10%
    - Number of recent credit inquiries
    - Time since recent account opening(s), by type of account
    - Time since credit inquiry(s)
    - Re-establishment of positive credit history following past payment problems.

5. Types of Credit Used 10% A FICO® score takes into consideration all these categories of information, not just one or two. No one piece of information or factor alone will determine your score. The importance of any factor depends on the overall information in your credit report. For some people, a given factor may be more important than for someone else with a different credit history. In addition, as the information in your credit report

changes, so does the importance of any factor in determining your FICO® score. Thus, it's impossible to say exactly how important any single factor is in determining your score – even the levels of importance shown here are for the general population, and will be different for different credit profiles. What's important is the mix of information, which varies from person to person, and for any one person over time.

Your score considers both positive and negative information in your credit report. Late payments will lower your score, but establishing or re-establishing a good track record of making payments on time will raise your FICO® credit score.

What exactly does my credit score mean? There are three main credit bureaus: Experian, Equifax, and TransUnion. With a tri-merge credit report – a report containing a score from all three major bureaus – most lenders look at the mid score.

EXAMPLE: Experian, 720; Equifax, 657; Trans Union, 717

In this case, 717 would be the mid score. These scores represent a composite of the borrower's credit history, employment, ability to save, and so on. The higher your score, the better chance you have of receiving credit with a low interest rate.

EXCELLENT: 850-730     *     GOOD: 729-680

FAIR: 679-620     *     POOR: 619-500

NO FEDERAL FUNDING:     500 and below

**Frequently asked Questions about Credit repair**

<u>If the negative trade line is truly mine (not an error), can I still dispute it?</u>

Yes. Under the Fair Credit Reporting Act consumers can dispute the accuracy of a trade line if they question the validity of the lateness, collections, and/or public records reported. Most of our clients do not, in all honesty, know if they were late one time or five times. Therefore, they can honestly challenge the validity of the negative trade line. It is then our job to make sure that the three credit bureaus and the original creditors are reporting the correct dates and information.

## What items can legally be removed from a Credit Report?

Discharged bankruptcies, Charge-Offs, Collections, Credit Account Late Pays, Foreclosures, Inquiries, Judgments, Mortgage Lates, Notices of Default, Repossessions, Student Loans, Tax Liens, Identity Theft and Bankruptcy.

## What does CHARGE OFF mean?

If no payment is received on an account after 180 days creditors are required by law to charge off the account to receive their tax write-off. But, it's doesn't mean you don't still owe the debt, it's just been charged off.

## How does the seven-year clock work?

The seven-year clock begins ticking the moment a debt is incurred. Every time a payment is made, the clock resets itself. If no payments are made in seven years, the debt must be removed from your credit report regardless of whether it was charged off, sold, or in collections. This is the #1 reason why credit reports are inaccurate - debt purchasers and collection agencies keep resetting the seven-year clock (known as aging) in total disregard of the Fair Credit Reporting Act.

## Aged accounts must be removed from your credit report?

Creditors, collection agencies, and debt purchasers are required to validate debts and PROVE a payment was made which allowed them to reset the seven-year clock and most can't.

## What about "free" credit reports?

The "free" credit reports advertised on TV or internet are NOT free. They all want you to "sign up" for something that costs you money and offer merged credit reports that are the most pitiful excuse for credit reports we've ever seen – nothing but garbage.

## Federal Laws Creditors Don't Want You to Know

1. FAIR CREDIT REPORTING ACT (FCRA): Here is a summary of your major rights under the Fair Credit Reporting Act (FCRA). For more information, including information about additional rights, to www.ftc.gov/credit.

You must be told if information on your file has been used against you. Anyone who uses a credit report or another type of consumer report to deny your application for credit, insurance or employment or to take another adverse action against you must tell you and must give you the name, address and phone number of the agency that provided the information.

You have the right to know what is in your file. You may request and obtain all the information about you in the files of a credit bureau (Equifax, TransUnion and Experian). You will be required to provide proper identification, which may include your Social Security number. In many cases, the disclosure will be free.

You are entitled to a free file disclosure if: a. a person has taken adverse action against you because of information in your credit report. b. you are the victim of identity theft and placed a fraud alert in your file; c. your file contains inaccurate information as a result of fraud; d. you are on public assistance; and e. you are unemployed but expect to apply for employment within 60 days.

You have the right to ask for a credit score. Credit scores are numerical summaries of your credit-worthiness based on information from credit bureaus. You may request a credit score from the credit bureau that creates scores or distributes scores used in residential real property loans, but you will have to pay for it. In some mortgage transactions, you will receive credit score information free of charge from the lender.

You have the right to dispute incomplete or inaccurate information. If you identify information in your file that is incomplete or inaccurate, and report it to the credit bureau, the agency must investigate unless your dispute is frivolous.

The credit bureau must correct or delete inaccurate, incomplete or unverifiable information. Inaccurate, incomplete or unverifiable information must be removed or corrected, usually within 30 days. However, a credit bureau may continue to report information it has verified as accurate. Credit bureaus may not report outdated negative information.

In most cases, a credit bureau agency may not report negative information that is more than seven years old, or bankruptcies that are more than 10 years old. But the fact that they can report on a bankruptcy for a maximum 10 years does not mean your credit score can't be excellent.

Access to your file is limited. Credit bureaus may provide information about you only to people with a valid need, usually to consider an application with a creditor, insurer, employer, landlord, or other business.

You must give your consent for reports to be provided to employers. A credit bureau may not give out information about you to your employer, or potential employer, without your written consent given to the employer.

You may limit "pre-screened" offers or credit and insurance you get based on information in your credit report. Unsolicited "prescreened" offers for credit and insurance must include a toll-free phone number you can call if you choose to remove your name and address from the lists these offers are based on. You may opt-out with the nationwide credit bureaus at 1-888-5OPTOUT (1-888-567-8688).

You may seek damages from violators. If credit bureaus, or in some cases, a user of consumer reports or a furnisher of information to a consumer reporting agent violates the FCRA, you may be able to sue in state or federal court.

Identity theft victims and active duty military personnel have additional rights.

2. THE FAIR DEBT COLLECTIONS PRACTICES ACT (FDCPA) REQUIRES DEBT COLLECTORS (BUT NOT BANKS) TO: Identify themselves and notify the consumer that the

communication is from a debt collector and that any information obtained will be used to effect collection of the debt.

Give the name and address of the original creditor upon the consumer's written request made within 30 days of receipt of the notice.

Notify consumer of their right to dispute the debt. The 30-day notice is required to be sent by debt collectors within five days of the initial communication with the consumer. The consumer's receipt of this notice starts the clock running on the 30-day right to demand verification (validation) of the debt from the debt collector.

Provide verification (validation) of the debt. If a consumer sends a written dispute or request for verification within 30 days, then the debt collector must either mail the consumer the requested verification information or cease collection efforts altogether. Such asserted disputes must also be reported by the creditor to any credit bureau that reports the debt.

File a lawsuit only in a place where the consumer lives or signed the contract.

The following conduct is prohibited under FDCPA: Hours of phone contact: outside the hours of 8:00 a.m. to 9:00 p.m. local time.

Failure to cease communication upon request: communicating with the consumers in any way (other than litigation) after receiving written notice that the consumer wishes no further communication or refuses to pay the alleged debt.

Causing a telephone to ring or engaging any person in telephone conversation repeatedly or continuously with intent to annoy, abuse, or harass.

Communicating with consumers at their place of employment after having been advised that this is unacceptable or prohibited by the employer.

Contacting a consumer known to be represented by an attorney.

Communication with a consumer after a request for debt validation has been made; communicating with the consumer or pursuing collection efforts by the debt collector after receipt of a consumer's written request for verification of a debt made within the 30 day validation period and before the debt collector mails the consumer the requested verification or original creditor's name and address.

Misrepresentation or deceit: misrepresenting the debt or using deception to collect the debt, including a debt collector who misrepresents that he/she is a lawyer or police officer. Publishing the consumer's name or address on a "bad debt" list.

Seeking unjustified amounts, which would include demanding any amounts not permitted under an applicable contract or as provided under applicable law.

Threatening arrest or legal action that is either not permitted by law or contemplated.

Abusive or profane language used in the course of communication related to the debt.

Communication with third parties: revealing or discussing the nature of debts with third parties (other than the consumer's spouse or attorney).

Contact by embarrassing media, such as communicating with a consumer regarding a debt by post card, or using language or symbol, other than the debt collector's address, on any envelope when communicating with a consumer by use of the mails or by telegram, except that a debt collector may use his business name if such name does not indicate that he is in the debt collection business.

Reporting false information on a consumer's credit report or threatening to do so in the process of collection.

3. TELEPHONE CONSUMER PROTECTION ACT (TCPA) VIOLATIONS: The Telephone Consumer Protection Act of 1991 (TCPA) became federal law in 1991. The TCPA governs the conduct of telemarketers and debt collectors.

The TCPA restricts the use of automatic dialing systems (also known as auto dialers or predictive dialer), as well as artificial or prerecorded voice message, SMS text messages received by cell phone, and the use of fax machines to send unsolicited advertisements.

A consumer is unlikely to know if a call to his or her cell phone was initiated by using an auto dialer – they will sound like any other phone call. A call imitated using an auto dialer may have a live person on the other end. However, in order for a debt collector or telemarketer to maintain a volume operation, they must make thousands of phone calls each day – so, if you are getting calls from a debt collector or telemarketer on your cell phone, there is a good chance they are violating the TCPA.

Examples of Common TCPA Violations: Unless a consumer has previously given express consent, it is generally a violation of the TCPA for a business to engage in any of the following conduct:

Calls made to your cell phone, which were initiated by the use of an auto dialer.

Calls made to residences, which were initiated by an artificial voice or prerecorded message.

Call made to your cell phone, which were initiated by an artificial voice or prerecorded message.

**Five Steps to Rebuild Your Credit**

**Step One:** File Bankruptcy (please consult a bankruptcy attorney if this is the right step for you in your life). The first stop to re-establishing your credit may be to file bankruptcy. Sometimes in life, you have to take a step back to take a step forward. Although a bankruptcy may be reflected on your credit report from seven (7) to ten (10) years, this doesn't mean that you can't reestablish your credit immediately after your case is completed. In fact, many creditors regard you as a better credit risk after you file bankruptcy simply because your debt has now been eliminated but you still have the same earning potential as before. Additionally, since you will not be able to file another bankruptcy for eight (8) years, lenders may perceive you as a good candidate for future credit. Consequently, there are many lenders who now specialize in providing credit to people who have just completed their bankruptcy. It is not uncommon for our clients to receive credit applications in the mail immediately upon the completion of their case. Obviously, any new credit should be taken out responsibly and managed properly so that you can maintain a healthy financial outlook. We are amazed at how quickly our clients can rebound from their bankruptcy. Many of our clients now enjoy a much more carefree lifestyle with new homes, vehicles and very little other unsecured debt.

**Step Two:** Live within a budget and use cash for all your spending needs. There is a common misperception that people who file bankruptcy have misused their credit or spent carelessly. In our experience, a person's spending habits have little, if anything, to do with why they filed bankruptcy. Eight out of ten bankruptcies today are triggered by unexpected medical bills, illness, unemployment and/or divorce. Most of the people we meet who require our services do not have a problem with spending; they just have experienced a rough patch in their life, which sent them into a downward financial spiral.

Notwithstanding the above, bankruptcy provides you with an opportunity to wipe the slate clean and start again financially. In this regard, it is a good opportunity to reassess your financial priorities and outline a budget to maintain a healthy financial lifestyle. You may have to sit with your family and discuss your financial goals. We recognize that this may not be easy considering the social, cultural and emotional pressures upon American's middle class. But now is the time to reprioritize your finances.

Budgeting takes determination and discipline. Controlling spending and saving money are essential after bankruptcy. There are many subtle changes you can make to your spending habits to save even just a few dollars a week. Many people can reduce their monthly expenses by simply avoiding impulse buying, paying cash for things and preparing more meals at home. There are also many ways to reduce fixed monthly expenses like insurance and transportation costs.

**Step Three:** Start a savings plan. Have you heard the old adage that cash is king? Well, it is true! Money in the bank is one of the most empowering and inspiring feelings after emerging from a bankruptcy. Since your debts are going, you should be able to save a little bit each month as long as you stick to your budget. Use the money you have been spending to make minimum credit card payments to start a savings account for yourself. It doesn't have to be much. It's okay to start small. Write yourself a check every month for half of the amount you were sending to the credit card companies. Or even one-tenth of that amount. You won't even miss the money if you start setting it aside NOW.

A savings account at a bank isn't your only option. Check into whether your employer has a 401K program or other retirement plans available or start your own individual IRA account. That way you are less likely to spend it. In addition, you may want to explore investing small amounts into mutual funds, CD's or other low risk investment options.

**Step Four:** Review your credit report. Often, credit reports contain negative entries that don't belong there or are incorrect. It is important that you review your credit report after your bankruptcy to ensure that all your debts are reflected as discharged and that your credit score is accurate. If you discover inaccuracies with your report, you may challenge them and the reporting agency will correct your file if the information cannot be verified.

**Step Five:** Obtain new credit. Many people worry that they will never be able to obtain a credit card again after their bankruptcy. Other people are glad to be rid of credit cards and swear that they will never touch a piece of plastic again. No matter how you feel, credit cards provide you a valuable way to rebuild your credit history after bankruptcy. By rebuilding your credit history, you can qualify for the same low interest rates on home mortgages and car loans as other people do.

You can typically obtain credit if you demonstrate a consistent employment record and signs of financial rehabilitation. Most people find that if, after filing bankruptcy, they promptly make the payments they are left with, such as car payments, house payments, and rent or utility payments, they can re-establish their credit soon after filing bankruptcy. Another opportunity to rebuild your credit is by obtaining a secured credit card. In order to obtain a secured credit card, you are required to deposit a certain amount of money with the bank offering the card. Then you are able to use the card like a regular credit card up to the amount held on deposit by the bank. Secured credit cards offer similar credit benefits as bank loans. In addition, credit unions are an excellent source for car loans after bankruptcy.

Finally, it is very likely that you will receive several unsecured credit card solicitations immediately upon the discharge (completion) of your bankruptcy. Accept a few of these applications, but use the credit wisely. If you use a credit card during any monthly cycle, then make sure that you are in a position to pay it off in full. Anytime you have a remaining balance, which carries into another month, you are headed in the wrong direction and warning lights should go off in your head to once again step back and regain control of your spending.

By using your credit card and paying it off in full on a monthly basis as we suggest, your credit score will start to improve dramatically. You will be surprised how little credit you actually need. If you utilize credit intelligently, you can make the system work to your advantage and start the process for a healthier financial lifestyle.

## 15 Tips to Re-establish Credit and Raise Your Credit Score

1. Correct your credit report within one month of receiving your discharge of debt from the bankruptcy

2. Never co-sign for anything - especially family members.

3. Never share your bank account with anyone - no exceptions.

4. Get a secured credit card from a local credit union. They will require a deposit of between - $300.00 to $500.00 but it's worth it. Always pay early and always pay more than the minimum payment.

5. Never pay off your credit cards - always keep a small carry over balance to establish a good payment record.

6.  Open a checking or savings account. Lenders may look at this to determine if you can responsibly handle money.

7.  Apply for store and gas credit cards where you would normally pay cash.

8.  Apply for a secured card where you deposit cash and charge against it.

9.  Pay your utility bills and rent on time for at least a year.

10. Find a friend or relative to cosign for you on a loan and pay it on time.

11. Look for car dealers and mortgage brokers that attest to be "bankruptcy friendly." Buy a used car, so you do not get hit with the depreciation that occurs during the first two years of a new car purchase.

12. Stay away from payday loans that are at high interest rates and are a "bad credit" trap.

13. Live within your means. Do not unnecessarily increase your debt to income ratio by taking on credit to purchase luxury items that you DO NOT NEED. Your payments on consumer debt should equal no more than 20% of your expendable income after costs for housing and a vehicle.

14. Pay your reaffirmed, pre-bankruptcy debts on time.

15. Close your EBay and PayPal accounts! Neither EBay or PayPal extend credit to their members, yet both randomly pull members' credit reports without written authorization, which will lower your credit score. EBay Inc. also shares your personal info with their entire corporate family (all subsidiaries worldwide), their vendors, etc., etc., etc., thus substantially increasing your level of risk for identity theft by leaps and bounds.

**Bankruptcy Lender Friendly Credit Cards**

The following is a list of credit card companies that offer cards to consumers after bankruptcy. The list contains both secured and unsecured credit cards. This list is in no way exhaustive, but should be a good starting point for rebuilding credit!

In addition, there are a number of credit card search companies on-line that can help find credit cards to suit your financial situation. Most of these services cost money, but usually their fees are refunded if they cannot find you a credit card.

There are also a number of "stored value" credit cards that are similar to secured cards, except they do not require you to put any money into a bank account right away. You deposit money on the card and use the card up to the limit of your "deposit" into the account. You can find most of these by searching the internet. Most of these types of cards have applications that can be completed on-line.

SECURED UNSECURED

First National Bank of Marin, Orchard Bank/Household Bank, 1.888.338.8406 / 1.800.477.6000

First PREMIER Bank, 1.800.987.5521

Cross Country Bank Secured Visa, 1.800.252.1159

Orchard Bank/Household Bank, 1.800.477.6000

Use this information to get the life you have worked hard to get and improve. Remember, don't take your newly obtained good credit for granted, as ID theft is the fastest growing crime. Check your full credit report at least quarterly to ensure that you have not become a target.

# Chapter 2

# Identity Theft & Protection

## By Vivian Gaspar

Why would a thief break into a security-enabled home when all they really need to do is to go through your mail box, your garbage, or just find your name in the phone book or on the internet? Today's **identity thief** is one step ahead of outdated laws that are ill-equipped to punish today's technology-enabled criminals.

Here are some basic facts:

- 1 in every 10 U.S. citizens has already been victim

- 47% of victims have trouble getting credit or a loan as a result of becoming a victim of ID theft

- It can take up to 5,840 hours to correct damage from being a victim – That is just like being in jail for 8 months!

The unfortunate fact is that authorities simply do not possess the resources to pursue identify theft as vigorously as more intrusive crimes like, say, burglary. Wait a minute! Isn't identity theft considered burglary? Well, yes, Virginia, there is a Santa Claus. And while Santa may be apprehended while breaking into your home, he will not be held for going through your mailbox. Identity theft, after all, is burglary, and is every bit as intrusive. As stated above, our modern-day criminal is one step ahead of our legal system. All said, while our current laws offer limited or no protection against identity theft, there are measures that you can take to safeguard your identity.

Due to the extreme inundation of illegal aliens committing this crime it is unfortunate that according to Arizona Border Defenders website:

"Illegal aliens may enjoy a free pass on identity theft due to a new investigative policy at California's Department of Motor Vehicles." You might be saying to yourself. That is in California, why should I care? True, however, this can unfortunately become a precedent for all other state courts to refer to.

## *"Of Debits and Credits"*

Debit and credit cards are increasingly the preferred method of payment for transactions big and small. Knowing the rules as they apply to your bank and the type of account that you have is paramount to protecting yourself. Be "in the know" when it comes to the rules of the road regarding your accounts.

> **Best Practice:** *Favor the use your credit card over your debit card for regular monthly purchases and pay it off in full at the end of each month. Monitor your ratio of 'used' versus 'available' credit, keeping the ratio at 30% where possible.*

Many banks require that you argue a fraudulent **debit card** transaction within seventy-two hours in order to get reimbursed. This window extends to thirty days for **credit card** transactions. This should be a no-brainer. Using your credit card for common purchases, then paying it off monthly is a best practice that will give you the time window to actually receive and scrutinize your monthly statement; then to report any fraudulent activity that may occur. Using a credit card for all transactions makes good *risk management* sense. Paying the card off completely at the end of each month (to maintain availability for the next month, while not incurring unwanted debt) makes good *financial* sense, as it will minimize finance charges. Finally, the regular monitoring of 'used' versus 'available' credit on your account makes good *credit* sense, as it will assist in keeping your credit score as high and as healthy as it can be.

An additional precaution: Maintain a minimal balance in the account attached to your debit card and keep the majority of cash in your savings account. This strategy removes the majority of your liquid cash from "the front lines" while adding a layer of complexity to any would-be thief attempting to access your cash or identity. This is just an added strategy to aid in your overall risk management approach to protect yourself and your assets.

Now let's talk about other areas of identity theft. Did you know that…

a) …to obtain your address, today's modern-day thief need only perform a reverse-lookup of your phone number, if you receive your phone bill at your home? (This is especially true for your cell phone, which is often the number which you give to stores for your membership discount and the person behind you can easily overhear you.) Remember, this is a very common tool for stalkers as well. Keep your home address safe and do NOT receive your phone bills to your home address, not only to protect your identity but your family's safety as well.

b) …to obtain your social security number, today's modern-day thief need only input your name, using an <u>incorrect</u> social security number, into a software program. The program for this will then return a message stating that the information which you provided is incorrect; then will provide that person with the <u>correct</u> information. Voilà! Your social security number, on a silver platter.

c)  ...to obtain your credit report, today's modern-day thief need only use your name and address. As you may already know, the personal credit report is the golden gateway to a smorgasbord of personal information including, but not limited to, current and past addresses, previous employers, credit card information, and more!

d)  ...the modern-day, technology enabled thief in each of the above cases need not be a thief at all! It can be anyone on the street, including (and most likely) an overly aggressive marketing company. Why, you ask? Because obtaining the above information is not illegal! Using the acquired information for nefarious purposes may be illegal, but this is a gray area at best.

In three simple steps, a would-be thief (or aggressive marketing company) could have your name, address, phone number, social security number, and credit report. It sort of reminds me of the children's show, "Agent Oso," where Agent Oso solves problems in "three special steps." I now picture my three year old pulling up social security numbers and credit reports in three special steps (in between watching Elmo and playing with his Thomas trains, of course). Life isn't quite that simple for ordinary honest folks; why should pulling your private information be made so simple for the dishonest and for corporations to obtain?

> **Best Practice:** *For roughly $20 per month, obtain a P.O. Box or the like (UPS Store, Mailboxes Etc.) for all your bank and credit card statements, and phone and utility bills. This is an excellent risk-management practice against the intrusive forces of the universe. It also provides a personal security safeguard against would-be stalkers that may overhear you giving out your phone number (think, "reverse lookup"). The author of this chapter has maintained a personal UPS Store address, for this very purpose, for ten years now.*

**Shred!** I know everyone should have heard this one by now, but it should not go unmentioned: Shred, shred (and shred!). Shred everything that you put into the garbage that has any personal or account information. Did you receive an offer of credit, membership, video or book of the month club in the mail? They contain personal information. Shred them!

Rather than discontinue shredding due to your fifth paper jam in twenty minutes, all because you saved money by purchasing the cheap shredder, do yourself a favor – get the good model shredder! Putting a premium on your personal information and safety by investing in a good shredder will save you aggravation, especially when the paper jams. So invest in a good shredder; it will be well worth it in the long run.

## The "S" is for *Security*

When shopping on the Internet look for the "s" added to the "http". The "http**s**" signifies that you are now on a secure website. Also, always use a credit card for added security when shopping online.

Remember, even though it might not be fair, you will be judged on your credit score and the contents of your actual credit report in everything from your car insurance and homeowners insurance rates to background checks when you apply for a job. So protecting your credit is really more critical than most people realize, especially when that job you have been praying for is on the line.

## 7 More Basic Steps to Protect Your Identity:

- Review your Nationwide Criminal Records Report

- Review your drivers record report from your local division of motor vehicle department annually. Remember, the thief can steal your driver's license information which can result in your getting your license suspended, having your insurance rates increased or getting cancelled or you can even get arrested if the thief commits a crime in your name.

- On the signature line on your credit cards put: "Ask for photo ID"

- Review your Medical Information Bureau file annually – got to www.MIB.com (free once a year)

- Ensure no one else has filed taxes in your name by reviewing your IRS transcript annually. -800-289-1040

- Sign up for SSA electronic payments with IRS before a thief signs up in your name. 800-772-1213/www.ssa.gov

- Stop pre-approved credit offers: www.optoutprescreen.com / 888-567-8688

Last, but definitely NOT least, and most importantly: know that by law, many of the places that request your social security number are not entitled to it. The reason they ask for it is that in the event you do not pay them, they will have the ammunition to collect from you more easily. Some of the most common companies that request your social security number on forms (remember, we have been conditioned to complete forms without question since our school days) include: your doctor, dentist, hospital, any medical office, cable company, phone company, your children's school and camp. Just the other day, I went to my doctor and they asked me to complete their form which requested my social security number, so I politely told them I do not provide my social security number to medical providers and they were fine with it. That is because they know that are not entitled to it. They are asking for it anyway from whomever will provide it. One of the most frequent ways ID theft occurs is when a medical provider has a data breach. You cannot stop a data breach, but you can prevent them from having your social security number in the first place.

Remember to do what is in your power to protect your identity because it can cost you hundreds of hours and thousands of dollars to recover it.

# Chapter 3

# Debt Settlement

## By Rocco Sileo

I am going to share some information about credit card companies and credit card debt that most people do not know or choose not to believe. If you or anyone you know has either fallen behind or is struggling to keep up with interest payments, please read through this section carefully, as you may be able to help yourself or someone you know to potentially save thousands of dollars!

Did you know that an individual with just $10,000 in credit card debt, making minimum payments with the national average interest rate of 19%, would take 58 years to pay it off, with almost $29,000 of additional interest? Isn't it convenient that most credit card companies give you a minimum payment just enough that you can afford it? They have a goal to get you on the treadmill and redirect your money into their pockets. They make you feel good about things by giving you frequent flyer miles and patting you on the back while they smile and pick your pocket slowly but surely over a lifetime!

These companies have been killing people softly for many years and when consumers can't pay anymore, they cut their losses and move on to the next steady paying profit center (consumer). The part that should interest you is where I mentioned "cut their losses." What does that mean?

Most people pay their bills if they can afford them. Often circumstances change and people can be forced into a bad spot if there is a decline in household income. The dreaded word bankruptcy comes to mind when we think of the only way out. But that is not the only way to eliminate debt by any stretch. Debt settlement was flying under the radar for years and only those who took the time to research options took advantage of settling for less. Most creditors are willing to significantly reduce outstanding balances if a consumer is struggling. I've seen settlements as low as fifteen cents on the dollar lately! Nowadays, you can hire a professional law firm to assist in this process. By using a law firm, the reduced amount may be paid back over time (usually three or four years). The consumer's monthly outlay is often cut in half of the normal required monthly interest expense. The point is that a person can get a cheaper payment to get out of debt compared to what it's currently costing them to stay in debt!

You should be asking, "What's the catch?" Simply put, a consumer must be struggling in order to get help. This is not going to work for those that have assets. In fact, the net worth of a consumer may have an impact on taxable income for forgiven debt, so be sure to confirm with your accountant as well when looking into this option! A consumer must either be unable or unwilling to continue paying the minimum payments (an example of an unwilling person may be someone on a fixed income with no disposable income left over after the interest on the credit cards is paid). Yes, this will lead to late marks on credit reports and possible judgment filings as public records in some cases, but is it really all that bad? First, most candidates for debt settlement don't have strong credit to begin with, and when only minimum payments are made every month, regardless of pay history, the credit score will go down a little further leading to the slow death of a credit rating. A judgment will prevent a consumer from having clean title until the account is settled. So as long as there are no major purchases or sales needing to be made until after the accounts are settled, it shouldn't be a huge factor in the decision making process.

Compared to bankruptcy, a debt settlement plan has far fewer long term ramifications. Through the settlement process, a typical consumer will have a few late payments that turned into collections or judgments and were eventually paid. Settled accounts are easier to remove from a credit report and have less of an impact on a consumer's score than a bankruptcy. The example below offers three different options available to a consumer who is struggling with credit card debt and looking for a solution.

John and Mary have $10,000 in credit card debt with a 19% interest rate. John and Mary live paycheck to paycheck, and after all living expenses are paid, they can only afford to make the minimum payment of $350 each month. What options are available to them?

1. Continue to make the minimum payments for the next three years and hope things eventually pick up. This option would cost $12,000 in interest payments and the balance would still be $10,000 owed at the end of three years.

2. Find the up-front money to file bankruptcy. This option can cost a few thousand dollars in some states, just to hire the attorney! Then, just hope that there is no forced repayment of any kind, and that the public record never prevents the consumer from getting a job. Also realize that it will take a long time for the public record to come off the credit report.

3. Enter a settlement plan and repay only about $5,000 total spread out over 3 years ($138 per month). Deal with short term credit ramifications and have disposable income left over at the end of the month to establish a saving.

I'm not suggesting that settling for less is always the best route to take. But what I do know is that knowledge is power! The more information a consumer has at his or her disposal will usually lead to making better decisions. Debt settlement has undergone some regulatory changes and there has been plenty scrutiny as of late in the industry. Much of the bad press has been due to both propaganda from the credit card companies and a few bad players in the industry who misled consumers. I am advising consumers to do their homework on their personal situation and on the company or law firm that they are considering using to get help if they choose debt settlement. Find out the fees and when they are taken before signing a contract. The option to negotiate on your own is always available if someone has the time and knows what they are doing.

# Chapter 4

# Bankruptcy Basics

## By Santo Bonanno, Esq.

Due to the economic crisis since 2007, bankruptcy filings have doubled. Approximately 98% are individual filings vs. corporate. For the first time, many other attorneys are sending clients to bankruptcy attorneys. The bankruptcy laws in New Jersey changed in 2005 and the requirement for the attorney's due diligence for their liability. This change took place because large credit card companies complained to Congress, which then made changes such as requiring individuals to take a credit counseling course. The course must take place before filing, and a financial management course must be taken before obtaining the discharge. This is a new federal law.

Bankruptcy is a federal law and someone has the right to elect if it benefits them. As one more extreme case, Florida has a homestead exemption state law which means the debtor (individual) can choose to keep the home regardless of the amount of debt as long as their mortgage is paid.

Bankruptcy is fairly universal in the laws and exemptions

throughout the US. The most common causes for filling have been 1) loss of job 2) divorce 3) disability. The formula is if a person's debt is greater than $20,000, they file for bankruptcy; if the debt is less, then settlement is sought. The reason for the $20,000 guideline is that federal law allows each debtor to keep $15,000 of assets from creditors for their fresh start. The general cost for filling bankruptcy is $2,000 for Chapter 7 and $3,000 for Chapter 13.

The types of bankruptcy available for individuals are:
Chapter 7, Chapter 13 and Chapter 11: All 50 states require the attorney to disclose their fees on the petition; anything that is beyond the initial retainer must be approved by a bankruptcy judge.

All trustees are attorneys who are full-time attorneys, but part-time trustees, who receive a flat fee for each case they handle, paid to them by the US Trustees' Office.

The most common type of bankruptcy is Chapter 7, which is commonly called straight liquidation. It is used by individuals who have less than $20,000 in assets. In New Jersey, the exempt assets are: 401k, IRA and pensions, as an example. Therefore, the $20,000 in assets can be above and beyond the aforementioned exempt assets.

Chapter 13 filings are for those who have more than $20,000 in assets and wish to protect them. This is done by giving the creditors between 5%-100% repayment plans based upon ability to repay, which is not to exceed 60 months. The payments are done through a bankruptcy trustee, who in turn pays the creditors at a 10% commission, which the trust gets for their service. The Chapter 13 trustee is appointed in each jurisdiction by the US Trustee Office. Jurisdictions are based on populations with no less than one per state.

Chapter 11 is for those individuals whose assets or liabilities exceed $650,000. Liabilities are the creditors. It operates the same as Chapter 13; however, instead of paying a trustee, you pay directly to your creditors. The cost of filing a Chapter 11 is a minimum of $1,050 + the attorney's retainer, which starts at $5,000.

Business owners can only file Chapter 7 or 11 if it is a corporation. Chapter 13 filing is only for individuals who have less than $650,000 of debts and assets.

How does a business owner close a business where they have signed personal guarantees? They must first file for a business Chapter 7 for both their corporation and for themselves personally if they have signed any personal guarantees for corporate debt such as in the most common cases, corporate credit cards, leases or corporate lines of credit.

In a Chapter 7 filing of bankruptcy:
The trustee will do a liquidation analysis on all real estate owned by the debtor. This is usually just for the primary residence. The trustee will get an appraisal, which is paid for by the debtor; then 10% is subtracted for closing costs, which covers real estate commission and transfer tax, then all mortgages against the property are subtracted, and lastly the Federal personal real estate exemption of $20,400. If there is no equity left after that analysis then the trustee will abandon the property and you may keep your home as long as the debtor works out an acceptable mortgage modification with the mortgage holder.

If there is equity above the liquidation analysis, and you wish to retain the property, you can negotiate with the Chapter 7 trustee to buy out the equity or a portion of the equity so that the trustee will abandon the property.

~ What may be a surprise to many is what may be included in dischargeable debt: mechanics' liens and judgments, as well as 1040 IRS debt over three years old, as long as neither was deemed to be fraud.

~ In a Chapter 13 filing of bankruptcy:
As long as the debtor makes the payments into the approved plan to the Chapter 13 trustee, the home cannot be foreclosed upon. This type of bankruptcy stops any foreclosure process as long as the plan is approved and complied with.

*Mortgage modification can* be used with any type of bankruptcy at any stage prior to sheriff sale, which is the enforcement action of a foreclosure.

How does bankruptcy affect divorces? Bankruptcy does not eliminate child support, alimony, or any other provision of a support order that is entered by the matrimonial court.

Non-bankruptcy debts are as follows:
- Sales and use taxes
- Federal withholding taxes if you are an employer
- Income taxes that are less than three years old and the returns have been filed
- Domestic support orders
- Injuries caused by drunk driving
- Any debt which was caused by fraud or misrepresentation
- Criminal fines and restitution

# Chapter 5

# Getting Yourself to College

## By Stacey Plichta Kellar, Sc.D.

I am a college professor and I am here to tell you that getting a college degree from a public or non-profit college is one of the best things you can do for yourself, your income and your children. Lots of studies show that, compared to people who did not go to college, people with a college education are[1,2,3] :

- healthier and live longer
- more satisfied with their work
- more likely to be employed
- making more money than people without a college education.

If that is not enough incentive, when you go to college you will also benefit your children. The best way to teach is by example and your children are much more likely to do well in school and then to go on to college if you also go to college.[4] In fact, some studies show that you can have an even greater impact on your children by increasing your educational level after you have your kids!

It doesn't matter how old you are, how long it has been since you have been in school or even if you tried and had trouble in college the last time – there is an option for you! Many students who I have advised come to me saying that they are worried that they are 'too old' to start a degree. The truth is that you will get even older, with or without a college education! One of my close friends took 15 years to finish her teaching degree. She took 1-2 classes a semester while raising her children and working outside the home. It took time, but she just got her first job in the classroom and she is really happy! Many of my Master's and Doctoral students started out getting a two-year degree at a community college.

It can be scary to think about going to college, especially if your parents did not go. I know that college campuses can be intimidating and many students are nervous the first time they enter a classroom. Don't be scared. College is fun. You will get to meet a lot of interesting people. College classes will give you something interesting to think about. College will also help you get the skills you need to move your career forward, to change your career or to start a new career. Most importantly, going to college will give you a boost of self-esteem and confidence like almost nothing else!

## A Word about Online Courses and Online Degrees

Online courses are a great alternative once you are on the path to a college degree. Most public community colleges and four-year schools offer a variety of fully and partially online courses. However, the personal touch is always better and you want to have a professor physically available to meet with you – at least at the start. As a returning student, you will be more likely to get the help you need if you have a physical campus that you can actually go to for assistance. Online courses also take more self-discipline – it is really easy to let the work go when you don't have to actually show up to class, and it takes time to develop study discipline. Many community college students who take online classes wish that they could take fewer online classes than they currently take. Additionally, most employers prefer job applicants with a traditional degree, rather than with an online degree.[5]

## Starting Out? Choose a Community College

There are so many college choices available to you – but I am going to recommend that you start with your local community college. Yes, there are also public four year schools, non-profit four year schools and the for-profit schools – most of which are online. It is important to start school in a way that leads to success. The best way for most of you to start your college experience is to go where you will get the personal attention and support that you need to succeed. If you had a bumpy road on your last try at college, the community college is the place that can help you navigate your way to success. You want to make sure that you pick a public community college and NOT a for-profit alternative – I'll talk about why in the next section.

Why a community college? Most of you are probably working adults who are thinking about going back to school. It has probably been years since you have been in a classroom. Additionally, I'm sure that many of you probably have a job, are raising children, and you might be helping to take care of a parent as well. Your local community college is the place that is best set up to help you balance your new venture in college with your busy life.

The many advantages of a public community college include:

- Lower cost. The tuition at public community colleges is about one-third of public four year colleges and MUCH less expensive than the for-profit colleges.
- Professors that focus on teaching. Professors at community colleges are often more accessible to students and can spend the extra time with students who need it.
- Smaller class sizes. Four-year colleges can have class sizes with hundreds of students! The typical class size at a community college is 25-35 students.
- A chance to improve your skills. If you need to brush up on English or math before you can take a college level course, a good community college will offer you courses to help get your skills brushed up and college ready.

- Support services. The mission of community colleges is to help students like you succeed. They offer numerous low-cost or free support services including tutoring, skills workshops, academic advising and career planning. They also offer excellent support for students living with disabilities.
- Many programs to choose from. Most community colleges have a wide variety of programs that you can choose from. You can also try classes from different programs before settling on a major.
- It is easy to take your education to the next level. The course credits from community colleges will transfer to most four-year universities. Community colleges often have articulation agreements with the four-year state colleges and universities. These agreements allow you to use the credits from your two-year degree toward a four-year degree if you decide to continue your education.

## Which Schools to Stay Away from?

I would recommend that you stay away from the online and for-profit schools, at least at the start of your education. The problems with the for-profit schools have been well documented – including in a U.S. Senate Report from an investigation launched by Senator Tom Harkin (Chair of the Senate Committee on Health, Education, Labor and Pensions (HELP)).[6] These problems include sky-high tuition, students being saddled with large amounts of student loan debt, low degree completion rates and companies simply seeking to make a profit. In short, the majority of students who start at these online for-profit schools leave with a lot of debt and no degree. The Huffington Post also has a series of articles that discuss the challenges of for-profit colleges (http://www.huffingtonpost.com/news/for-profit-universities/).

## How to Pick a Community College Using College Navigator

The federal government, through the National Center for Education Statistics, offers a great tool for choosing a school. The website, http://nces.ed.gov/collegenavigator/, provides you with a national search engine to find schools in the U.S. It also has a lot of great information about college tuition and financial aid. To find a community college near you, start by entering your ZIP code in the box that says "ZIP Code" and then enter how many miles you are willing to travel to school. Under "Level of Award," choose "Associate's." Under "Institution Type," choose both "Public" and "2-year." This should bring up the list of community colleges that are near you.

When you get the list of community colleges that are near you, spend some time exploring the websites of each college. When you are ready to proceed, go to the Admissions page of the college website. Most of these will give the office hours and a contact phone number. You can call and ask to speak to an admissions officer. They can answer all of your questions and help you get started with the admissions process – including financial aid. The admissions officer is a really important source of support for you as you start the process of going back to school. Additionally, most colleges will host "Open-Houses." If you can possibly go, this is a great way to learn about the college and what it can offer you.

## How Much Will Community College Cost?
The most cost-effective way for you to get a college education is to pay the 'in-state' or 'in-county' rate at your local community college. The cost for a year of school, going full-time, is listed in "College Navigator." A full-time student is typically one who attends school at least 12 credits (roughly four classes) per semester. The typical cost of community college tuition for one year is approximately $2,600. Of course, this varies greatly by region. In my area (Northern New Jersey) the tuition cost for one year of community college as a full-time student is $4,185. As a comparison, the tuition for one year at the local "for-profit" school is $17,181.

Since you are most likely going to go part-time, it makes more sense to look at the "per-class" cost, rather than the cost of going full-time. Most classes are three credits and also have associated fees, so it takes a little math to figure out your total cost. For example, at the community college near my house, the tuition for in-county residents is $118/credit. Additionally, there are some mandatory fees, including a $20/credit College Fee, a $12 technology fee and a $7 registration fee. So, the total tuition for one three-credit course would be (3*$118) plus 3*$20, plus $12 plus $7. This equals $433.00 as the total cost for one course.

In general, public community colleges will offer the least expensive way to go back to school, and the best value for your money as a returning adult student. In addition to low tuition, many offer partial scholarships and all offer assistance with applying for state and federal financial aid. For more information on college affordability, see the U.S. Department of Education's College Affordability and Transparency Center: http://collegecost.ed.gov/catc/. Here you can get a sense of the highest and lowest cost options available to you.

**Financial Aid and Scholarships**
The full cost of a two-year college degree is, on average, around $5,200. This is, of course the cost before you take into account any financial aid you might get. Every college is different in the type of scholarships and grants that it offers. This is where an admissions officer can be of invaluable help to you. However, there are some commonalities to almost all forms of grants and financial aid. The base of most financial aid is the FAFSA – the 'Free Application for Federal Student Aid'. The deadlines vary by state, but the website usually opens up in March and some of the deadlines are as early as March 1st for the following academic year (an academic year is September-May). The website for the FAFSA is: https://fafsa.ed.gov/. You will need to have a bunch of information ready, including your birth date, social security number, federal tax returns and bank statements.

Once the FAFSA is complete, your school will receive the results about one month later. You may also be asked to provide your college with additional information. After the Financial Aid office has all of the information that it needs, it will put together an award package for you. This package will consist of a combination of Federal, State and Institutional grants and scholarships. There are three types of student aid:

- Grants: These do not have to be paid back.

- Work-study: You work a certain number of hours in return for aid
- Student Loans: These have to be re-paid, with interest, when you are finished with school

The financial aid officer at your school can explain these to you in greater detail, as your options will depend upon your personal financial status.

**Getting Started**
The best way to get started towards a college education is to decide that you want one and to move forward with your decision. Visit the College Navigator and look for schools near you. Go to visit the schools on their Open House day. Go have lunch on campus. Get comfortable being on campus. Get to know the Admissions Officers at the school you are interested in. Take one course as a non-degree student just to try it out and see if the school is right for you.

I know that people worry a lot about the cost of a college education, but it doesn't have to cost a lot. Tuition at public schools (e.g. state colleges) and even some of the non-profit schools is quite affordable. You can take one class at a time if you need to. There are also federal and state programs to help pay some of the costs of college. The college where I work is a public institution, and almost 80% of our undergraduates finish with no debt at all (http://cuny.edu/about/resources/value/savemore.html)!

**References**
Because I am a college professor, I wanted to show you, my readers, that everything I am saying is evidence-based. The research articles below provide the evidence for everything I said in this chapter. When needed, I included the web-links to sources that help to explain what the articles are saying in plain language. Please take a look!

[1]Buckles K, Hagermann A, Halamud O, Morrill MS, Wozniak AK. (2013). The Effect of College Education on Health. Working

Paper 19222. National Bureau of Economic Research Working Paper Series, Cambridge MA. http://news.nd.edu/news/41300-college-graduates-healthier-than-non-grads-study-shows/

[2]U.S. Department of Education, National Center for Education Statistics. (2014). The Condition of Education 2014 (NCES 2014-083), Labor Force Participation and Unemployment Rates by Educational Attainment. Accessed on 9/14/2014 at: http://nces.ed.gov/fastfacts/display.asp?id=561

[3]Pew Research Center. (February, 2014). The Rising Cost of Not Going to College.
http://www.pewsocialtrends.org/2014/02/11/the-rising-cost-of-not-going-to-college/.
A short version is at: http://www.pewresearch.org/fact-tank/2014/02/11/6-key-findings-about-going-to-college/

[4]Choy, S (2001). Students Whose Parents Did Not Go to College: Postsecondary Access, Persistence and Attainment. Washington DC: Department of Education, National Center for Education Statistics,NCES 2001-126.
http://nces.ed.gov/pubs2001/2001126.pdf

http://everydaylife.globalpost.com/education-level-parent-affect-childs-achievement-school-6869.html

[5]Public Agenda. (September 2013). Not Yet Sold: What Employers and Community College Students Think About Online Education. A Taking Stock Report.
http://www.publicagenda.org/files/notyetsold_publicagenda_2013.pdf

[6]U.S. Senate, Health, Education, Labor and Pensions Committee. (2012). For Profit Higher Education: The Failure to Safeguard the Federal Investment and Ensure Student Success. Majority Committee Staff Report and Accompanying Minority Committee Staff Views.
http://www.help.senate.gov/imo/media/for_profit_report/PartI.pdf

# Chapter 6

# Get Educated for Low to No Cost

## By Darsi D. Beauchamp, Ph.D.

College expenses are on the rise in the 21st Century. Nonetheless, college can be free for many if they qualify. It all begins with good marks in high school. By having a good standing and a good grade point average (GPA), a student can be eligible for many programs. One such program is NJ STARS. A student must be a resident of New Jersey and must be in the top 15 percent of their graduating class. The Edward J. Bloustein Distinguished Scholars scholarship is for high school seniors who will attend an approved college or university.

Scholarship or grant monies are available to use in studies in different areas, such as health care, law enforcement, teaching, accounting, sciences, etc. Each college and university has their own scholarships and/or grants. The Free Application for Federal Student Aid (FAFSA) must be filled out *every year* by each student; otherwise you may not be considered for financial aid. In addition, state universities (in New Jersey for example) such as Rutgers State University, Montclair State University, The College of New Jersey, Kean University, New Jersey City University, Ramapo College,

Richard Stockton College, Rowan University, Thomas Edison State College, and William Paterson University have more scholarship and grant opportunities than private colleges.

Needless to say, county colleges also have a lot of opportunities. In addition, county colleges offer a variety of approved two-year programs at lower costs than four-year universities. County colleges can also be a saver; in other words, the two-year colleges can be cost effective in the first two years of a Bachelor's degree. Make sure the courses are approved by the four-year college you want to attend. County colleges offer a variety of courses both during the school year and the summers that can count towards any major at a lower cost. In addition, when you attend a two-year college and then apply at a four-year college you will be considered a transfer student. This means that you are not competing with the general population, but only with yourself and this allows you better chances in getting into a four-year university with only two more years to pay for. During this time, a person who takes courses at a two-year college has the ability to do well and maintain a higher GPA. The higher GPA will help you get into honor societies and receive scholarship or grant monies as well to go into the four-year university.

Furthermore, many foundations exist which provide monies based on need or merit. These foundations have criteria and deadlines that must be strictly adhered to or your chances to qualify will decline.

There are foundations that are based on the area of study or just based on your heritage and even on your name. The choices are endless and millions of dollars go unclaimed every year. The monies are available for undergraduate, graduate, doctoral programs, and post-doctoral (graduate) programs. There are many websites that can help you begin your quest; you may begin with this one and continue to search state and federal and specific school scholarships and grants.

http://www.studentscholarshipsearch.com/Scholarships/Local_Scholarships/United_States_Scholarships/New_Jersey_Scholarships/more2.php

If you are unemployed, check with your reemployment agency for a review of your skill set. The agency may be able to retrain you in another area. Grant monies are also available to attend approved schools and are paid for by the Department of Labor and Workforce Development.

# Chapter 7

# What is Time Management?

## By Arnold Rintzler

Is your desk covered with tons of work to be done, projects to review, and letters that require a response? Does your "To Do" list seem to grow longer and longer regardless of your efforts? Do you ever feel overworked, underpaid, and unappreciated?

Or, is your energy level at an all-time high? Do you always finish your work before you leave, and find yourself able to give each project or person ample attention? And finally, are you spending enough quality time enjoying your family, friends, and personal hobbies?

If you have ever had a day in which you felt as if you worked hard with long hours and still got nothing accomplished, you need to get organized. If important matters are regularly pushed aside so that you can put out a fire, or address a crisis, you need to get organized. Does a life filled with personal and professional achievements, with plenty of time to relax and enjoy the fruits of your labor – and above all, living *your* values and *your* goals – describe *your* life? Or does this seem like an unattainable dream? If you, like many other people, have let your life get out of control…relax. Regaining control and living a life that provides you with tangible and intangible rewards is more achievable than you think.

In the rapidly changing, very time-conscious world in which we live, effective time management is important because it provides a necessary focus to help to get more done…with fewer people…in less time.

There used to be a great number of companies and time specialists that promoted and sold "unique" calendar planning systems as the answer to all of one's organizational challenges. Now we have gone to computers, smart phones and tablets, for the most part. Yet, you can still open almost any magazine that focuses on improvement and you'll find an article about time management. There are almost as many time-management "secrets" as there are weight-loss "secrets." Each promises you a magic formula to help you realize success with little or no effort. The fact is that success without effort is an anomaly, and there is no "secret" to effective time management. There are several techniques that can work, and it really doesn't matter if you use Google Calendar, Outlook, or a traditional paper-based system. **What matters is not what system you use, but that you use a system.** What matters is that you prioritize your activities and actions and set meaningful goals. And what really matters is that the system you use works for you…so YOU can achieve more in less time and have more discretionary time to enjoy the fruits of your labors.

Time management is a skill, a technique, a mindset, and a lifestyle. It can be learned by anyone who:

- has a desire to get more out of his or her life,
- wants to feel more in control,
- wants to achieve success in business while enjoying the pleasures of a personal life
- Wants to reduce stress and realize more balance in life.

While achieving effective time-management is not easy, and no habit change is, time management is a matter of replacing less-than-effective habits with better ones. It is fairly simple. In fact, you probably already have a head start!

The truth is that almost everyone has a fairly good understanding of the basic time management techniques. Almost everyone knows how to plan and prioritize. Most know they should be more organized. The problem is that very few of us always do that which we know we should do.

It is important that we have a successful Time Management System. Think in your mind about someone you believe is very successful. Does that person keep his or her word? The answer is probably yes. If we keep our word consistently, we create power in our lives. The more powerful we are - i.e. the ability to have things and events be the way we want them to be - the more effective we are. The more effective we are, the better we feel. What is the first thing we need to do before we keep our word? It is to give our word. That creates the POTENTIAL for us to keep our word, which in turn creates POWER for us to be effective and feel good, and therefore to be more effective. We call this "THE FORMULA FOR WELL BEING."

|  | P |  | P |  |
|---|---|---|---|---|
|  | O |  | O | Feel Good |
| Give Your Word | T | Keep Your Word | W | -------- |
|  | E |  | E | Effective |
|  | N |  | R |  |
|  | T |  |  |  |
|  | I |  |  |  |
|  | A |  |  |  |
|  | L |  |  |  |

## EVALUATING CURRENT BEHAVIOR AND HABITS

While there are ideas and techniques that have stood the test of time and will help you get more out of your time, one's primary focus should not be on external systems, "skills" and "knowledge." Rather one should focus on attitudes, internal feelings, and habits. Focus on learning how to harness the natural energy that comes when you are doing something that is exciting and meaningful to you. Focus on developing the mental confidence, empowering attitudes, and a life-planning process that will give you back control of your life and help you to live it in a fuller, richer, and more satisfying way. Achieving more, feeling better, and becoming more successful has more to do with your internal attitudes, self-esteem, goals, and aspirations than with external events.

If you attempt to change behavior through utilizing a new time management system, prioritizing in a different way, or any of the other available techniques without addressing the way you think and feel, who and what you value, and what your goals are, any success will be limited and short-lived at best.

## CREATING A STRONG FOUNDATION

Your behavior is influenced by your mental and emotional outlook, your attitudes. That's why developing healthy fulfilling attitudes is such a critical part of time management. Your ability to manage your time will be governed in large measure by your ability to manage your life. It will also be influenced by your goals, and how important they are to you. **In the end, Time Management is not a time management issue; it is a personal and professional goals clarification issue.**

In any change process we must examine the three keys to achieving higher levels of success and getting more enjoyment out of that success:

> #1 Attitudes –The foundation for success in any area is developing a success oriented attitude – about yourself and others. While this may sound like a trite cliché, the fact of the matter is that what you do is influenced by how you think, and how you think is founded in your most basic attitudes.

#2 Skills – Identifying, developing, and continuously improving the skills, both technical and non-technical, which we will utilize to achieve our goals is a critical link in the achievement chain.

#3 Goals – Both professionally and personally, goals provide direction and purpose to living a life filled with achievement, prosperity, and happiness. A successful life is a balanced life. Success is the continuous achievement of your own predetermined goals, stabilized by balance and purified by belief, in both your personal and professional life.

All too often, we live our lives as if we had an unending supply of days. Unfortunately, that is simply not the case. We are only here for a visit. Each of us has a certain number of days on this earth. While that number varies, one truism does not vary: some people get much more out of just a few days, while others seem to spend a lifetime accomplishing nothing. There are twenty-four hours in a day for everyone. Yet, some seem to accomplish much, while many take an inordinate amount of time to do little. For each of us, both of these phenomena periodically occur. On certain days we accomplish a great deal, and time just seems to fly by. All of a sudden we look at our watches and are surprised by the lateness of the hour. On other days, everything seems to be in slow motion. Minutes seem like hours, and hours seem like days.

The quantity of time doesn't really change. There are always sixty seconds in a minute, sixty minutes in an hour, and twenty-four hours in a day. What changes is not time. What changes is our perception, and perception is our reality. When we are having fun working at challenging and stimulating projects directly related to our goals, our achievement level skyrockets and time flies. When we are bored or doing something we don't like, we're constantly checking the time, which drags, as does our level of accomplishment. When we feel "under the gun," "behind the eight ball," and "out of control," time seems to go too fast. We feel out of control and stressed, unable to get done what we need to accomplish in the time allotted, and are forever behind on our projects. Since we cannot increase or manufacture more time, we must get more out of the time we have.

If we return to our original premise that almost all of us know how to manage our time, and that we realize the value of becoming more effective at managing our time, why don't more of us do a better job of doing so? We all know what we _should_ do. NIKE made famous the "Just do it!" slogan. For most of us, that's easy to say, but difficult to do. Why? To answer that question, we must first look at the factors that influence our behavior.

## ATTITUDES

Our behavior is influenced by our desires and our thoughts. The way we think is influenced by our attitudes. Our attitudes are developed through a conditioning process that began very early in life. These attitudes continue to be a dominant force in determining our success or failure in all areas, including our ability to manage our time and control our lives. By examining the future and the past, you will develop a much better understanding of why you do the things you do. This insight will help you to improve your ability to manage your time and your life, and to ensure that a full and rewarding future is your destiny.

We must begin by examining our early conditioning and existing attitudes. Before you begin to think about changing your attitudes, you must first examine the ones that you've already developed. Take the time to crystallize your vision and your values and as a result evaluate the effectiveness of your current attitudes. It is helpful to understand more about your existing attitudes and how and why you make some of the decisions that you make. It is also helpful to examine the effect early conditioning has on behavior and attitudes. If early conditioning was predominately nurturing and encouraging, a person is likely to mature into an adult who views trying new things with positive anticipation and has only a small degree of fear of failure. As a child, were you encouraged to try new things? Were your efforts recognized with positive accolades? Or were your attempts forgotten and your failures rewarded with admonitions and warnings? If your early environment and conditioning was supportive and encouraging, you probably find it relatively easy to accept new challenges. However, if your early conditioning was very judgmental, and you typically received harsh criticism for mistakes, you will probably tend to stay with the "safe" and "known" tasks where you know what to do.

If a person was raised in what many view as a "traditional" environment where early admonitions were the norm and "good manners" the benchmark, that person may avoid new challenges for fear of criticism or reprisal. Did you hear things like "Speak your mind regardless of who disagrees with you?" or (and more likely) did you hear, "Children should be seen and not heard!" or "Don't talk to strangers!" or "Don't go where you're not wanted!" and other negative admonitions? As a result, do you sometimes find yourself uncomfortable in new situations or hesitant to suggest a new idea?

If much of our early rewards as children came from doing everything we were told to do and that was what we learned that made us feel successful, and now we find that we cannot possibly do everything on our plate all of the time perfectly, is it any wonder that maybe we feel overwhelmed and NOT successful or in control?

## DEVELOPING TIME-CONSCIOUS ATTITUDES

The first step in changing *any* habit is to identify the habit that you want to change. This is true for your habits about time attitudes as well. Establish a period of time to analyze your attitudes, behavior, situations, and outcomes. Evaluate your present use of time. Recording exactly how you spend your time is an important discovery process. Most people have a very inaccurate understanding of just how they actually spend their time.

Create an accurate time analysis that will help you to pinpoint who and what occupies your time. To ensure accuracy, do not try to rely on your memory and attempt to "complete" your analysis at the end of the day. Keep it with you and note everything you do as you do it. Before you can control your time and develop better time management habits, you must understand or identify existing habits.

After you consolidate your data and evaluate your time use, look for activities that you may want to delegate or eliminate; look for time wasters, and peak performance periods. Pinpoint precise behaviors that are incompatible with your vision, goals, and values. For example, if your goals include getting a promotion that will mean an increase in salary, yet you keep making commitments to your friends and family that will keep you from excelling at work, your behavior is inconsistent with your goals. If your early approval was dependent upon doing for others, and you find yourself regularly taking on more than you can handle, your behavior is understandable, although self-defeating.

Examine your attitudes and to determine if a change in thinking is warranted. If your goal is to make more sales but you avoid sales-oriented activities, your behavior is inconsistent with your goals. If you want to achieve outstanding success, but you work minimal hours and exert only average effort, your behavior is inconsistent with your goals. You can either change your goals to be more inspiring and motivating so as to propel you to do more, or you can change your behavior by developing new habits of thinking and habits of doing.

It is important to define the new habit that you wish to develop. Be as specific as possible. For example, if you wish to develop a more balanced life and feel more in control, you might take a personal-development course that will help you to develop your skills in setting and achieving goals. If you want to develop habits conducive to success in business, you might read autobiographies of those successful in business, or participate in a personal development process.

Just as negative habits in our lives can be undermining and destructive, positive ones can be uplifting and forwarding of our goals. Building habits requires defining very precise behaviors and performing them at specific times, motivated by deeply held values. As Aristotle said, "We are what we repeatedly do." We can identify what we want to become and become it.

Be meticulous about your daily planning process. Plan tomorrow before you finish today. Both self-discipline and self-management are critical aspects of time management and both of these can be developed. Focus on your rewards.

Crystallize your rewards to yourself and make a note of them so that you are reminded of them often. Your rewards must exceed in value the price you'll pay in effort, or you will be inclined to revert to old habits. Once you decide to do something, make a promise to yourself to continue until you win! Keep your promises! Take responsibility for your own success or failure. Recognize the value of a long-term benefit rather than momentary gratification.

Develop a winner's attitude. Think positively about your opportunities, your potential, your ability to achieve your goals, and your right to success. Focus your thoughts. Train yourself to seek solutions and not to place blame, and to focus on that which you can control, and not on that which you can't. If you break an iron rod at its weakest point and weld it back together again, the weakest point becomes the strongest point. Your weaknesses, if faced head on, can become your greatest strengths. Don't run away from things just because you're frightened. If you do, you'll always be afraid.

# Chapter 8

# Goal Setting

## By Arnold Rintzler

Defining your purpose, establishing your values, and developing success-oriented attitudes will give your life meaning and will give you a sense of direction. It will not, however ensure success. Only goal setting, planning, and working your plan will do that. Your vision of the future you'd like, if turned into goals and taken through the proper planning process, can dramatically affect the quality and fullness of your life. Goal setting is a powerful tool for higher levels of achievement. However, goals are only as attainable as your belief in your ability to attain them.

Lofty goals set by someone with a lack of confidence are as realistic as building a skyscraper on quicksand. They will get swallowed up and lost in the muck and mire of daily survival. A vision of a future filled with happiness, achievement, and success, created by a person with a low self-image, is destined to remain an elusive dream. However, a clear vision of a successful future, fueled by passion and developed by a person with a positive self-image, is destined to become reality.

Goal setting and planning will help you manage your life as well as your time. Focusing on your goals and on the rewards must become a habit. To develop this habit, begin and end each day with a review (and a reminder) of your goals and what's important to you. Note your progress. Evaluate your priorities and carefully choose your upcoming activities.

Whether your objectives are great or small, you can achieve more of them more often by addressing these questions:

1. What do I want to do?
2. How can I accomplish this goal?
3. What steps need to be taken to get started?
4. What obstacles are in my way?
5. How do I overcome them?

Establish goals and priorities in both your business and personal life. Organize your time to ensure realization of goals in both areas. You will find forms for crystallizing both your personal and business goals in the appropriate sections. Getting organized and feeling in control will contribute significantly to a life filled with achievement and satisfaction. Establishing and working toward goals that are important to you will add excitement and meaning to everything you do.

You might want to ask yourself these questions:

- Does work become a source of fulfillment, a place and activity where many of your personal needs can be satisfied?
- Do you feel like your day is providing value?
- Do you recognize the importance of your personal life?
- Do you give your family, friends, and hobbies priority?
- Do you enjoy your leisure time?

- Do you plan time for personal improvement and relaxation?
  Do your personal goals include goals in all six major life areas: Mental, Social, Physical, Financial, Family, and Spiritual?
- Do they include short and long-range, tangible and intangible goals?

Your goals, both personnel and professional, should include "becoming" goals as well as "having" or "attaining" goals. One will affect the other. For example, if you want to "have" more money, chances are that you must "become" worth more. You may have to become better at your job, better at another job, or perhaps even in another capacity. If you want to "have" more time to spend with your family, you have to "become" more organized at work. If you want to "have" greater respect and loyalty from others, you may have to "become" more deserving of respect and loyalty. To have, you must become. It is always useful to remember that, in life, investment always comes before reward.

Many people go through life without ever identifying what they want, where they want to go, or who they want to become. They get so caught up in day-to-day living that they fail to decide what they want to accomplish. They wonder why they feel frustrated, never achieving anything significant. It would be in their interest to realize the difficulty of hitting something they've never visualized or returning from somewhere they've never been. People who have no goals have no direction. They go around in circles, always moving, but never arriving or achieving.

Look at yourself honestly and squarely. Ask yourself: "What do I want to do and who do I want to be?" Crystallize your dreams and goals. List all those things that you'd like to have, to achieve, to see, or to be. Continue to add to your list and review it frequently, noting those goals that you achieve.

When setting your goals, be specific. Make sure that you can measure achievement. Goals such as "increase sales," or "lower costs," are not nearly as powerful as goals such as "Create 10 new clients," or "lower costs by $100,000.00." Your goals should be realistically high providing a need to stretch to achieve them. The oft heard quote: "Man's reach should exceed his grasp, else what's a heaven for?" sums up much of the motivational power of goals that are high enough to excite us.

Crystallize your goals. Writing them down helps you to focus and enhances commitment. If you share them with others, you can increase your commitment. Goals should always have target dates. This helps to build urgency and to prioritize your day-to-day activities and projects. And finally, remember to balance your goals between your personal and professional pursuits. Plan time for both. Too much work or too much play can wreak havoc in life. Without balance, even the sure-footed stumble and fall. Consider the mighty Roman Empire. The ancient Romans climbed to greatness, conquering neighboring lands and people. But once a vast empire was built, stretching from Britain to the Orient, the hard work and perseverance began to wane. The scales tipped to too much celebration and merriment. Under Nero, Rome celebrated 176 legal holidays each year. Imagine…almost every other day was a day of leisure! And we all know what eventually happened to the Roman Empire.

To be successful does NOT require stress, overexertion, a meaningless personal life, failed relationships or a mercenary attitude. The person who enjoys his or her work, feels that he is doing something of value, and has other relationships, commitments, and activities outside of work that are seen as being of value, is a success. The healthy person has both a successful career and a rewarding personal life. This does not mean that, from time-to-time, one or the other may take a back seat for a short time. For example, the salesperson starting a new territory may have to put in 80-100 hour weeks for about six months. A new parent may choose to spend time at home bonding and caring for a new child. Later that same year, a parent may focus on work so that he or she can provide for that same child's education.

When setting your goals, addressing balance is key. Be sure that you have goals in your personal, as well as professional, life. Just as all sun and no rain make a desert, all work and no play make a dull life.

## STAYING S.M.A.R.T.

One way to test your goals is to run them through the SMART test. Goals should be **Specific, Measurable, Achievable, Realistically high, and Target dates should be established**. Once you have established goals and determined priorities, the daily decisions become much easier because you have set parameters. Being goal-directed is not an intellectual exercise…it's a way of life. Every meeting, every telephone call, every transaction is focused. You are constantly asking yourself: What's my goal…for this meeting…for this interview…for this day?

In the absence of clearly defined goals, everything becomes a crisis, everyone becomes a task-master, and everything becomes urgent. You fall into the trap of becoming reactive rather than proactive. In the react mode, you will feel pressured, stressed, out of control, and filled with anxiety. When you are proactive, you will feel in control and powerful. Feelings of satisfaction and achievement spur you on to even greater accomplishment. Anytime you find yourself in the react mode, evaluate your goals, focus on your vision, organize your work, plan your activities, and work your plan.

## STRESS MANAGEMENT

If you continue to accept more than you can handle, you end up with many balls in the air, lots of responsibility, and lots of things to do. You also end up feeling overworked, underpaid, and unfulfilled. These feelings conflict with the basic human need to be appreciated, to be recognized and rewarded, and to live a fulfilling life. By taking on too much (in the quest for self-importance), many people end up feeling pressured and then make mistakes. If you promise too much to too many, and find yourself unable to keep your promises you feel guilty. All too often, because you feel guilty, you promise even more, and feel even more guilt. The process diminishes your self-worth and causes others to be frustrated, and a vicious circle continues and grows. How do you stop? Decide to not dance anymore to someone else's tune! Refuse to accept more than you can handle or anything that's not compatible with your purpose and your goals. Redesign how your work is performed.

Ask yourself: "What am I trying to prove? Who am I trying to please? How much of what I am doing is because I choose, and how much is because I feel compelled to please others or to prove my worth?" Many people who take on too much are trying to show others that they are worthy. In their excessive need to please others, they deprive themselves.

Don't set yourself up to fail or create imbalance by taking on too much, or too much in one area at the expense of another. If you do, you will create stress. Stress is frequently self-imposed, because we fail to plan, we schedule ourselves to be in two or three places at one time, or we agree to complete projects in days that should take weeks.

What are the top five sources of stress in your life?

Which of these can you change by planning your activities differently?

For those that can't be changed, can you reframe the situation for a different outcome? For example: look upon your dealings with a demanding boss as proof that you can handle any difficult situation or person. If you can learn to view stressful situations as opportunities for growth, you will relieve stress by taking control and developing a new attitude. If you can't control the situation, your best bet is to control the way you regard the situation.

When someone comes to you with a problem that you don't have time to solve, or one that actually could be better solved by someone else, return it to them immediately. A suggestion like, "I'd like you to think about this situation and come up with several possible solutions and then we'll discuss the solutions," or "I will not have time to address this until I finish the current projects I am working on. Could someone else help you faster?"

If you have allowed yourself to get over-committed, you've got some choices:

1. Continue doing the same things you've been doing.
2. Work more hours.
3. Lower your goals and/or standards.
4. Delegate.
5. Improve your time management skills and work habits.
6. Make decisions based on your purpose and your goals.

Consider what is important and what you want to achieve in your life. Challenge anything that is not compatible with your goals and/or priorities.

## OVERCOMING PROCRASTINATION

In any endeavor, there are barriers everyone faces at one time or another. Perhaps the most common one is a stalling tactic that you may call upon either consciously or subconsciously, i.e., procrastination. You may remember it from your high school or college days, when students thought it was "cool" to "cram" the night before the big exam. You may recognize it in a spouse or relative who talks about Christmas shopping for months and then lets it all go until December 24th. And you may even take comfort in the fact that procrastination is a habit of the masses. One look at the post office lines on April 15th is enough to confirm that fact, as everyone tries to file tax returns before the stroke of midnight.

Procrastination is the habit of needlessly putting off things that we should do, or say we should do, now. Procrastination can be caused by negative attitudes or fear of failure. It can be rooted in our own inertia, or as a result of lack of planning. It does more than almost any other habit we have to deprive us of satisfaction, success, and happiness. More than two centuries ago, Edward Young wrote: "Procrastination is the thief of time."

In fact, procrastination is much more. It is the thief of our self-respect. It deprives us of the fullest realization of our ambitions and hopes. In business, it can even cause or contribute heavily to our failure. "He who hesitates is truly lost."

When things are put off until the last minute, we create pressure. Every step finds an impediment. We push ourselves into blundering by having to make hasty decisions and judgments, and it actually becomes harder to do things. Haste does make waste.

Herein lies the paradox. By trying to take things easy, we do not make them easy. We actually make things harder. The first step in overcoming the tendency to procrastinate is to understand why you behave the way you do, and what kinds of situations cause you to take action.

None of us needs to look beyond himself or herself for examples of how procrastination has thwarted our goals achievement. Do you remember postponing that report that you should have done Wednesday? On Thursday and Friday you found yourself loaded with important jobs, and had to work over the weekend to get it ready for that Monday morning meeting. Or perhaps you postponed visiting a sick relative only to hear that it was too late? Many salespeople have lost an account to a competitor because they put off deciding how to approach a difficult prospect.

No one escapes his or her quota of difficult or unpleasant tasks. It is often these unpleasant tasks that contribute most to our success. You will learn a great lesson when you realize that they will not fade away if you ignore them or procrastinate. Eventually it's best to roll up your sleeves and wade into them. We work more effectively when we create a habit of doing the unpleasant things first and getting them out of the way so that we can do the things that we like to do later.

Do not allow an obstacle or difficulty to become an excuse. Instead of "I'm tired, I'll do it tomorrow," try "I'm tired, and I'll just work for another half hour and then go to bed." Reward yourself **after** you've completed something. Instead of thinking, "I'll never get this done," allow yourself the coffee break or other time out that you want after completing one part of the assignment. Remember, the journey of a thousand miles begins with a single step.

You do not see listless or languid people at the top of the success ladder. As Samuel Smiles said: "People who are habitually behind in their work are as habitually behind in success."

As a general rule, it is wise to make decisions promptly and crisply rather than lingering over them. In a competitive world, timing is critical. By waiting for precisely the right time, you may be much too late.

The well-organized life and business leave time for everything – for planning, doing, and following through. To the procrastinator, time is like a taskmaster with a whip. To the organized, action-oriented person, that same amount of time is like a savings account where the interest keeps growing. You have the power and ability to manage your time, or to have it manage you.

If you are not where you want to be, or who you want to be, make different choices. You have the power to choose where you live, with whom you live, and how you live. You have the power to choose where you work, what you do, and the quality of your work. You choose your level of success or failure based on how you choose to spend or invest your time.

# Chapter 9

# Finding the Right Financial Advisor

## By Brian Cody, CFP

There's an old expression that goes... "inspect what you expect" and that expression certainly applies to watching your portfolio. The best way to find out if you're working with the wrong advisor is always to follow the money.

The biggest issue I see when someone comes to me after having a bad experience with a financial advisor, is that they didn't ask their financial advisor what he or she was getting paid while selling them a product. Certainly, you will want your finance advisor to make a living at his job. However, it has to be fair. Some advisors provide products or services that have high upfront fees. Two of the important aspects you need to be aware of are if the products or services have upfront fees and if so, what they are, and secondly, what exactly is the advisor's incentive to continue servicing you once he has sold you these products.

Another way to see if you're with the wrong advisor is by asking your advisor what they have done to educate themselves over the last two years. Have they attended any seminars or earned new certifications? All of us must constantly be sharpening our knowledge base to keep up with changes in technology, the markets, and regulations. Your advisor should be a life-long student.

Finally, a good way to determine if you are with the wrong advisor is to see how they treat you. If they don't return your phone calls in a timely manner, if they don't smile when they see you and express a strong desire to help you, you are probably with the wrong advisor.

Five attributes for a great financial advisor to replace the wrong advisor:

Look for somebody who is a Certified Financial Planner TM (CFP®) or a Chartered Financial Consultant® (ChFC®) – these are two of the toughest certifications to receive in the industry.

Look for a person that has been in the industry for at least 5 years. There certainly are great financial advisors who have been in the industry for a shorter period of time; however, since so many finance advisors fail out within the first five years, don't take the chance that you're going to be with the person that is not going to survive.

Look for an advisor who has been referred to you by somebody else. It's always good to have somebody else refer any professional. First, the referrer has vetted the advisor and second, the advisor has to provide you good service or he will look bad in front of two clients.

Find an advisor that's going to give you a plan. Before you have to pay anything, ask the advisor to tell you how your money is going to be invested, what's the likelihood of reward and risk, and how does it fit into the overall picture for your financial needs.

Try to work with a financial advisor that is with a reputable company. You're investing your hard-earned money with this financial advisor, and you would hope that there would be a solid organization backing your financial advisor's practice.

# Chapter 10

# Financially Surviving Natural Disasters

## By Terrence Coughlin, CPCU, ARM, AICA

Taking Steps to Ensure Your Homeowners Insurance Claim is Processed Smoothly and Quickly.

Nobody is ever really prepared when natural disaster strikes; however, the list below will help you be prepared in case of an emergency. A readiness plan will put you one step ahead of potential financial disaster:

**BEFORE AN EMERGENCY**

1) Verify that you have emergency phone numbers, including insurance and utility company numbers in more than one place, e.g., on your refrigerator, in your wallet, and programmed into your cell phone. Do not list any financial data that could compromise your account should it fall into the wrong hands!

2) Make sure that the electrical panel is properly labeled so that you can shut off electricity to specific parts of the home.

3) Know where your main utility shutoffs are located for Gas, Oil, Water, etc.! Learn how to shut them off and make sure whoever spends the most time at home knows this as well.

4) Have an evacuation plan for the house.

5) Make one of your New Year's resolutions to change the batteries in your smoke detectors on New Year's Day.

6) Think about getting a recordable smoke alarm. Some people believe that children are more likely to respond to the recording of a parent's voice telling them to get out of bed than to respond to the shrill sound of a smoke detector alarm.

7) Think about what can be grabbed on the way out before an event happens. Don't waste time during a crisis.

8) Scan insurance policies every year (this can be another New Year's resolution). Some policies are subject to subtle coverage changes. Scanning your policies will ensure that you have hard-copies when you need them. Scan a soft-copy to a disc or thumb-drive, or even cloud computing – scanning them to Google Docs or the like. Just make sure that a copy will survive if the house does not.

9) It is becoming more and more popular to scan important documents, photos and other paper belongings. There are many ways to back up these files offsite so that if the computer is destroyed your valuable "memories" will still be recorded and available to you!

## IN AN EMERGENCY

1) Ensure everyone is safely out.

2) Dial 911 once you are sure that your family and occupants are safe.

3) Turn off the utilities to your home.

4) Then you may move your belongings or cover the belongings with tarps, if it is safe to do so.

## AFTER THE EMERGENCY

- Call your insurance company's 24 hour claim line. Be careful of what you say. For example, if there is water in the basement, say exactly that. Do not say "Flood." Describe the condition and do not use general terms. Flooding is only if there is an inundation of surface water, instead of water running into the basement from a backup of sewer and drain.

- Be mindful of wording by saying "wind damage" or "storm damage"; keep it simple. Wait until you have a clear picture of the damage before using descriptive wording.

- Be aware of the deductible issues in your policy. Many policies have a higher deductible for windstorm, a named storm or hurricane and tornados. Mislabeling the condition could cost you thousands. Be aware of exactly where the National Weather Service said there were tornadoes versus areas that just had heavy wind and rain.

- Know your policy before calling in the claim! When describing the damage, be specific to your policy. For example, there could be limitations for "silver" versus "collectibles."

# Chapter 11

# How a Private Investigator Can Help You Get Money

## By Alexander Toia

The role of today's Licensed Private Investigator is vastly different from what you see in the movies or on television. This chapter will focus on how the role of the Private Investigator, or "PI," can help you in this economy. The value and benefits that a Licensed Private Investigator can bring to the table are listed below:

**Locating Assets**

Whether you are looking to locate the assets of a debtor (pre- or post-judgment), potential investor, pre- or post-divorce, or after the death of a loved one, PIs have the resources to uncover assets. Many people are unaware they have a legal permissible purpose to locate assets prior to obtaining a judgment if a debt is owed to them, or that when a loved one passes away, they have the right, as next of kin or executor of the estate, to locate unknown bank, brokerage, and investment accounts. On your behalf, a private investigator can find: real property (residences, vacation homes, rental properties), motorized vehicles (automobiles, motorcycles, watercraft, aircraft, recreational equipment), personal businesses, bank accounts, brokerage accounts, investments, and safe deposit boxes.

## Background Investigations

Before entering into a financial agreement with a potential new partner, a background investigation can help you save considerable money in the long run. Knowing their business, civil, and criminal history will reveal whether or not this is the person with whom you want to share your financial resources and business partnership. Hiring a nanny? Knowing the person you are considering leaving your children with for hours at a time cannot be measured in terms of their safety, security, and welfare. Carefully choosing the right individual and verifying credentials is paramount. And you would be surprised to find out how it can be relatively economical with a reputable investigator. Check the records of potential contractors prior to forwarding them an advance fee, ensuring that you are dealing with a reputable company, and knowing the principal's correct full name. Also, signing a contract that makes them personally liable, and verifying that their company is the safest way to approach your project.

Background investigations are very unique assignments and require private investigators that know how to apply your circumstances to do the job right. While basic investigative and research techniques are employed, the investigator must be highly skilled in assessing and analyzing information, as well as developing and following leads. Understanding your problem and properly preparing the investigation are the most essential elements of every assignment. Backgrounds include, but are not limited to, the following:

Address History
Business Ventures
Civil Litigation History
Criminal History
Driving History
Employment
Expert Witness Backgrounds

Investment Opportunities
Pre-Employment
Public Records
Reconstruction of Activities
Resume Verifications

**Finding Loved Ones**

Do you need to locate a child you gave up for adoption, or are you looking for your biological parent(s)? Do you have a medical necessity to find either? Whether you need an organ or bone marrow transplant, or your family medical history, a private investigator can help find lost family. As a Licensed Private Investigator in the state of New Jersey, I had an assignment to locate a client's daughter who was given up for adoption 45 years ago at the tender age of 15. Through my efforts, I was able to locate the daughter with only a first name and date of birth, and arrange a meeting for her and the client. Other services include reuniting old high school and college friends and military buddies.

**Establishing Residency to Prove Co-Habitations**

When questions arise about how much money you are paying a former spouse in alimony or child support, clients like to know if another person resides there without your permission. If your ex-spouse is residing or cohabitating with an adult, you may have justification to decrease the amount you are paying in support. Private investigators can look for evidence to prove the permanent residential arrangement, which could significantly benefit you financially. In New Jersey, for example, if a former spouse is cohabitating with another person, same or opposite sex, you may file a motion and request your payments be decreased or terminated throughout the term of that relationship. As a Licensed Private Investigator in the state of New Jersey, I was able to save a client more than $450,000 by showing that his ex-wife had been living with a female partner for many years, even though she claimed to reside alone.

## Estates and Wills

There are several important reasons an investigator is hired in probate of a will or when a person dies intestate (without one). Heirs must be identified and located in order to probate or legally process the document. If the person dies without one, a reasonable effort must be made to find next of kin in order for the County Surrogate to release the deceased's personal assets. When people die in questionable circumstances, or as a result of an accident, family members, insurance companies, and estate lawyers might want to know what events precipitated, caused, or contributed to the death. If a person was unduly influenced, or of unsound mind, to execute a new will, such as a holograph (handwritten and legal), which could supersede an existing legal document, there would also be grounds for investigation to determine relevancy. While investigators cannot legally evaluate legal competency issues, we can still interview people that knew the deceased and can testify to his mental condition and behaviors prior to death.

## Electronic Bug Sweeps

When you suspect that your adversaries, opponents, and rivals may know too much about your professional and personal lives, it's time to sweep your location. A private investigator can help locate illegal listening devices and "bugs" in your home, workplace, vehicle, or telephones. Investigators can also inspect your car for GPS (Global Positioning System) tracking devices, which are generally uploaded to satellites while you drive and monitored by computer in real or post time. Additionally, trained and experienced PIs can inspect your hard drives, not only on your computer, but also in your cell phone. As a Licensed Private Investigator in the state of New Jersey, one of my cases involved the checking of a computer and cell phone pertaining to a suicide case that produced evidence to question the validity of the death.

## Pet Investigations and Recovery

Similar to lost loved ones, investigators use the same skills and techniques to find lost pets. As a Licensed Private Investigator in the state of New Jersey, in one of my cases a client's 12 year old dog was stolen by people that had a conflict with the elderly couple. Since they had no children, their dogs were treated as their offspring. The lived on a large piece of property where their five dogs could roam, and their prized possession was seized because of a disagreement. The staff of our company pitched in and contacted people they knew in the media. The Star Ledger, Daily Record, and Channel 7 Eyewitness News in New York City picked up the story and ran with it for a week. The clients offered a $2,500 reward for information leading to the safe return of their beloved pooch. Two people came forward with information that resulted in the reunion of the dog with the family. The clients were so elated they gave each of these people $2,500 and threw a party for 100 people at their home. This is a true story, and I have the news video to prove it!

# Chapter 12

# Acing Your Next Job Interview

## By Joanne Lucas

So, when does your interview start? Is it when you meet the employer? Is it when you set the appointment? Or, is it when you apply on line?

Your interview starts when your future employer or recruiter sees your information for the first time. It can be your resume, Facebook page, LinkedIn profile, or other public information. Whatever the source, you want to represent yourself well to future employers.

Let's start with your resume. Check your e-mail address. It should be: FirstName.LastName2015@abcxyz.com. Check that your e-mail represents yourself professionally. Keep your personal one (although future employers can see that one on your social sites), and get a free one with your name. That way, you will know when you have business e-mails and you will present yourself as a future employee.

The same goes for the message on your phone. When I call, I don't want to hear music, I don't want a "message," I just want to leave a message. One theme throughout this will be to make it easy for the person who may hire you. I understand that your child is cute. Save the message and re-install it after you get a job. And, if there is someone at your home who can't take messages accurately, please ask them to let all calls go to answering machines. That way, you will get the message accurately. I have been hung up on many times because the person answering the call can't take a message. You'll never know how many interviews you've missed.

Have paper and a writing utensil near the phone. Answer calls professionally. Be ready to interview. When you're looking for a job, your job is getting a job. So, when an employer calls to set up a meeting, be prepared to offer, "today or tomorrow." If people tell me that they can come in next week, I ask them to call then. I know that they won't and I have just saved time.

Dressing appropriately is important. You want the interviewer to remember what you can do, not what you wore! That means not a lot of cologne, nothing short, tight or low cut. And, shoes shined, shirt pressed and wearing a suit that fits. Limit jewelry to one or two pieces. Keep your interview outfit ready at all times. No one will know that you wore it the previous day.

When you go to the interview, show up 15 minutes before your interview time. Go alone! If someone needs to drive you, let that person stay in the car. Unless an ambulance comes for you, the longer you're there, the better it is.

Make friends with the Gatekeeper. That may be the receptionist or administrative assistant. Have some small talk ready. Have your smile ready. You will be amazed at how many people have lost jobs because they had an attitude with the Gatekeeper. That person will be on the phone as you're on the way to meet the interviewer. That information will either get you a long or short interview.

In the same vein, if asked to fill out an application, fill it out. Writing "See resume" will only show that you're not following directions and that you take short cuts. The application will have the exact dates, to whom you reported, salary and reason for leaving... all very important information to the target company. Please know that the application is a legal document. Be sure that your information is correct. Also, remember: Your favorite four letter word is "Open." Use it when asked for salary. You will write your previous salary, so they will know where you fit in their salary range.

If you were earning more and are willing to take a cut in salary to work for this company, be prepared to overcome that objection. Companies have hired candidates who have taken a cut, been trained, and then left to take their previous salary. It is very expensive for a company, both in actual costs, as well as morale, so they need to be as sure as possible that it won't happen again.

Also, bring reference information. Your company closed. Does that mean that you have no references at all? Do your homework. Find people who worked with you. Written letters are OK, but how many times have you heard, "You write the letter, and I'll sign it." Phone numbers or e-mail addresses show that you have prepared for the interview.

Speaking of preparing, with today's internet, there is no excuse to have no information about the company and the industry that it's in. Be sure to have questions to ask. You may write them down (it shows that you prepared).

One of the worst things you can do is to have no questions. One of the questions you may hear is, "Tell me about yourself." The interviewer doesn't want to know personal information. He/she wants to know how hiring you is going to help the company. Have your "elevator speech" ready. "This is what I've done, this is how I've helped, how can I help you?" At this point, you will hear what the responsibilities are and you can tell that person how you can do that and help the company at the same time.

If you're asked if you have any questions, answer in two ways: 1) I saw on your website that... or when I Googled your business... I found that... how will that relate to my responsibilities? 2) Ask questions as if you have the job... what will be the composition of the team that I will be on... where will I get the information on new products or services?

The interview is a sales opportunity, and the sale doesn't happen unless asked for. So smile, lean forward and tell the interviewer that you'd like to work there, and ask what the next step is. An employer wants to hire someone who wants to work there. This is a time to be positive. That doesn't mean saying that you're staying until you get an offer. When asking for the job, you have a great chance. If you say you're not leaving until hired, they call security.

If you're asked "illegal questions," what do you do? If you think about it, the only thing that the employer wants to know is if you're going to be there. Answer their concern. Go through the interview. Then assess if it is a place where you want to work. You still have control of your future. The company may be naïve as to questions that may be asked, or they can be a place to run from. But, without going through the entire interview, you won't be able to make that decision.

If asked about salary, the best way to answer it is to do your homework, and know what the salary is for that opportunity in your part of the country. "I'm looking for a good opportunity. I know you'll be fair." They will have seen what you were making in your last position and unless you were grossly underpaid or if you're taking a pay cut, they will continue when your salary is within their range.

If offered the job on the interview and you want it, TAKE IT! If you're not sure, just say that it sounds like a good opportunity and you'd like to think about it overnight. You'll know on the way home if it's the job for you. Two weeks only lets the employer know that you will take the job if nothing better comes up. No one likes to be second best. It's not a good way to start a job.

If you're looking for more money, plan your conversation for the next day. State what you're looking for and be sure to explain how you will benefit the company. Know that your salary has to fit in with the department. An extra $5,000 may mean a raise for the others in the department (people DO find out), and that may not be in the budget.

Give them a way to give you a raise if you meet certain guidelines. "If I can bring in the project in three months and under budget, can we discuss a bonus or a raise?" Many times that can be a positive because you will be bringing a value to the company. However, be prepared to either accept the job or turn it down at that time based on that conversation.

Send two kinds of Thank You notes. An e-mail thank you is great for instant gratification. A hand written snail mail will show your follow up skills. If it's between two people and you send the note, you have a good chance of getting the offer. All business is based on follow up. If you show that before you're hired, it's a good indication of future performance.

When you start a new job, make friends with people who LIKE working there. You can always find malcontents, but why do that? I'm sure that even at Microsoft there are unhappy people. As my husband says, "You need to be happy 10 minutes a day. Five minutes on the way to work and five minutes on the way home." If you can do that, you have it made and you have taken the next step in your career.

## Chapter 13

# The Right Answers for Those Tricky Interview Questions

### By Joanne Lucas

Be prepared. Nothing makes a more memorable impression to a hiring manager than a candidate who is prepared. Sounds so simple, yet too few job seekers take the time for simple preparation. When you follow these simple preparation steps you will have a leg up on your competition. There has never been a time when getting information was easier. Here is your check list for being prepared for your next interview:

- ✓ Look up the company's web site. (Prepare a list of interesting facts to mention during the interview.)
- ✓ Look up the industry on Google.
- ✓ Check out the company on LinkedIn.
- ✓ Check out the person you are interviewing with if you have their full name.
- ✓ Check out the company's competition.

- ✓ Look at people with similar positions in that department / company.
- ✓ See what their experience was before they started there.
- ✓ Find out what their specializations are.

The more information that you have, the better you will do.

There are also the standard interview questions which can trip up even the most professional job seekers unless they know the right way to reply. Here are some insider tips on how to answer the most commonly asked interview questions:

1) The one question that people dislike is "Tell me about yourself". They don't want to know that you like to ski. *What they want to know is how <u>hiring you will help them</u>.* People hire people who can help and solve their issues...not just do. You answer should be, "This is what I've done, this is how I've helped, how can I help you?" Listen to the answer, and describe how you can help in that area. That will help you focus on what the actual needs.

2) If asked, "Do you have any questions?" the correct answer is NEVER "NO"! Here are example questions to ask and comments to make to exemplify your interest and intelligence.

   a. "I saw on your website that"....
   b. "I was impressed by"...
   c. "I understand that the trend in your business is"....how does that relate to what I will be doing?
   d. What are your goals for me in my first 30, 60 and 90 days? (ALWAYS assume that you will be hired!).

Your job is to get the job, not to decide if you want it. "I'd like to work here...what is our next step?"

A great question to ask the person interviewing you is "What do you consider my strengths and weaknesses"? That's a WIN-WIN. If there is no weakness, that's great...what's our next step? If there is a weakness, there is at least a chance to overcome it. Not knowing about it doesn't make it go away.

Some employers may ask what you consider "illegal questions." You can say that, but you could and probably should just leave. BUT, you can answer the CONCERN, NOT THE QUESTION! In my experience the illegal questions are really asking WILL YOU BE HERE!

If it is are you married? Do you have children? How old are you? They are just asking if you will be there to work and will be there after training.

As to salary, the best course of action is for you to put your accurate salary on the application. When asked what salary you desire, the best answer is "I'm looking for a great opportunity. I know you'll be fair". If asked again then consider replying, "I'm currently earning, I'm looking for a great opportunity, I know you'll be fair." If you ask for too much then you won't get an offer, and if you ask too little, that is what you will get. Do your research on what that position should pay if you are not very experienced in your industry. You can do research on websites such as www.salary.com as a guide.

Good luck on your interview.

# Chapter 14

# How to Get Your Recruiter to Focus on You

## By Joanne Lucas

I'm a recruiter, and I want your attention!

I have been a recruiter since before fax machines, which means that I have spoken with many candidates as well as employers.

My job is to help employers attract and retain outstanding candidates in the Administrative, Finance, Sales, Customer Service, IT, as well as office arenas. I do that by finding people and by having people find me for the opportunities that I'm working on as well as the ones that I can create by marketing the experience of a candidate to an employer that I know can use that experience.

Although times have changed with the job boards and social networking, I still get referrals and ask for people with similar experience to people who they know can do a job.

How do you stand out? Have a resume that states what you have done and how you've helped. Return phone calls. Give information and take and use information to help you get the job that you desire.

And please be aware of your e-mail address -- that can be the first thing that people think about you. Be professional and simple. Do not use e-mail addresses with cute phrases and nicknames.

When you call me about an opportunity, please be prepared to speak about it. The job number doesn't help me. I understand that you're flexible, but be prepared to tell me how your background fits the opportunity.

Please apply for the jobs that you can DO! I know that you're a quick learner, but offices are so lean today, that they need someone who can hit the ground running. Also, do your homework. Find out about our company and the people that we usually work with. In other words, do your homework. Show me that you will research my client and that you are prepared to make a change.

When is the best time to get to know a recruiter? When you don't need one. It's like banks that only like to lend you money when you don't really need it. When a recruiter calls to tell you about a great opportunity and asks who you know that is qualified for that position, talk with him/her. If you do know people, refer them. You will be doing a friend a good turn. If it sounds like an opportunity that is interesting to you, be available to spend time with the recruiter as well as the employer. You may not be able to talk at work. We understand that. But we DO need to talk.

A friend may have heard about future layoffs, or may not have received the promotion promised, or not received the raise that was expected. Your friend may not tell anyone due to either embarrassment or thinking that no one can help. By introducing your friend to a recruiter, you will be doing your friend a service – if not for now, but for the future when knowing a recruiter is important.

A lot of people are happy where they are (we all know unhappy people... taking that unhappiness away will REALLY make them unhappy). A great candidate is someone who is happy in his/her job, but if a great opportunity were to come up would take it and start with two weeks' notice. That is the candidate that I like to work with.

Get to know and trust the recruiter. Know that when he/she calls, there is something important to discuss... if not now, sometime in the future. I've spoken with candidates who tell me that they don't need a recruiter. But, then the impossible happens and they don't have any place to turn.

OK. Now that you have a recruiter that you trust and that there is an opportunity that sounds interesting... now what?

Be a part of our team. Make it easy for us to get to know you. Give us the information that we need to be able to present you to our client. We are on your side! Our client is the company – the company pays our fee, but unless you're happy, it's not going to work.

We give you all the information that we have about the company, the particular hiring authority and what, in particular, they're looking for in their new employee. We're doing that so that you will do well on your interview. If we suggest a particular part of your experience to focus on, then please focus on that part. We know that you get nervous, but we're doing the best that we can do to help you do well on the interview and get the new opportunity.

If a resume needs to be "tweaked," please do it. We will never ask you to state that you did something that you didn't do, but will ask you to add what you have done. That piece of information may help an employer decide to hire you. We will talk about Counter Offer with you. Please read up on whether taking one is a good idea. When a candidate comes to me and says that everything about a current position is perfect except for... before I work with him/her, I recommend that he/she go to the employer and see what can be done to fix the problem.

Of course, there is no mention of leaving, or that if the problem isn't fixed, you will leave... that may help the "leaving" happen before you want it. But, if you feel you need a raise, bring in the numbers that you have to show how your work has helped the company. Have you increased efficiency? Created a new way to process orders? Worked with customers who were unhappy and solved the problems to keep the client? Employers give raises because they need you, not because you need one.

After that, if the employer cannot fix the problem, we can work together. My job isn't to get you a raise unless it's with my client. I don't want to waste anyone's time with a candidate who really doesn't want to change jobs or doesn't want to work. Of course, if you do get a raise with your current employer, that's great for all... you got what you want, the employer keeps an excellent candidate, and I haven't wasted anyone's time.

Please tell me any situations that may come up that would keep you from accepting and starting a job... vacations, other offers, time to be vested, bonuses and profit sharing. Surprises don't work well with us.

On an interview, your job is to get the job, not decide if you want it. Do your homework. Come prepared with answers to questions that you will be asked as well as questions for you to ask the hiring authority. Research the company; research the industry and competitors. Know what is happening in the business to know how your experience will best help the company.

Practice answering the questions. One question that people don't like is the "Tell me about yourself" question. How do you answer that? It is NOT personal. Remember it's like a trial... your lawyer will only ask what the opposing attorney can question. A company shouldn't ask about children, but, once you bring them up, the topic is fair game.

The answer to that should be, "This is what I've done, and this is how I've helped. How can I help you?" The interviewer will give you the main points that are required, and you can tell him/her how you can do it. Is there anything easier than that? That is also the "elevator speech" that everyone should have. That 60 second introduction should be an introduction that leads to questions and interest.

When asked if you have any questions, the answer should be in two parts: 1) "I saw on your website that... ." Hit them on the head that you did your homework. 2) Assume that the job is yours, "When I do this... who will get the results? What is my main goal in the first 90 days?"

An interview is a sales opportunity. You MUST ask for the job. "I'd like to work here, what's the next step?" And... just sit there and smile. Don't add anything until the interviewer says something.

The last questions will get you quite a bit of information. Ask: "What do you consider my strengths and weaknesses?" That is a win-win for you. If the interviewer can't think of any weaknesses, then ask for the opportunity again. I'm glad to hear that. I'd like to work here. What's our next step?" If there is a weakness, at least you have an opportunity to overcome it. Not knowing about it doesn't make it go away.

After the interview, call me as soon as you leave the interview. I can't talk with the employer until I speak with you. I can only believe that you're not interested if I don't hear from you. You may not get the offer for the job, but if you work with the recruiter, you will get another chance. Make the recruiter look foolish for sending you, and that will be the only interview that you're sent on.

We also stay in touch after you start. We love good news...so please let us know when you really like your new job. We also need to know if there are problems. But, PLEASE don't call us when you know that we won't be there, and PLEASE don't email us bad news. We can work with you through problems, but we need to TALK. I can't help you unless I know the problem and can help find a solution. "No news is good news" is NOT the way to start a new job or the way to work with a professional recruiter.

Remember us when others that you know are either looking to hire or change jobs. If we've helped you, please let others know. How to work with a recruiter? Work WITH us and the result will be positive!

# Chapter 15

# Direct Marketing: A Real Income Alternative

## By Camille Re

A legitimate and viable home-based business solution that is frequently overlooked is Network Marketing, commonly referred to as Multi-Level Marketing, or "MLM" for short. Network Marketing has received its fair share of negative press over the years; however, one would be hard-pressed to find an alternative with a lower cost and as low an overhead as an MLM. The role of the MLM deserves special mention in this book.

The first MLM started back in the 1950's with Amway. Amway was the first company to put together an MLM compensation framework. After Amway came other MLM entities replete with their own variation of the MLM model. Examples of these include; Mary Kay Cosmetics, Avon, Pampered Chef, Lia Sophia, Tastefully Simple, and the list goes on. Many people have made successful careers from these companies while others have made just extra part-time income depending, of course, on how you build and market their system. I have been a distributor for a few of these organizations in the past as my children were growing up, so I am familiar with different compensation plans, what to look for and questions to ask. Over the past 25 years I have never given up on my belief in the power of building a home based business. Home based businesses give you time, freedom, and part- or full-time hours, with minimal start-up costs, potential tax advantages, and little downside. Additionally, the possibility to earn a residual six figure income is very realistic, with the right effort of course. When you join an MLM you have the opportunity to not only make money from the products that you sell but from the sales of other representatives – the people below you – your downline. The person above you who signed you up is your direct upline.

When performing research on a potential MLM company, do not rely on pumping the company name into Google or other search engines. You will immediately reach the search result entitled, "Scam." MLM's are not scams, so please do not let someone else's failure dictate your future success or failure. Do not rely on non-credible sources for your research. Perform research but make sure that it is fair and unbiased. A good research tool is the company's own financial report. See how long they've been in business and how many quarters of growth they have.

Good advice would be to see what you are getting for your start-up. Know the risks. Do they take back products? What training and support can you expect? Set expectations with your upline. Find a company that will work with you, teach you and have a good return policy with little risk.

Some characteristics to look for when deciding on an MLM organization are as follows:

### Apprentice Program
This is a program whereby you may join the company with no money down. Apprentices usually start out as commissioned sales reps, where the commissions are banked within the company until you are able to fully join. Apprenticeship organizations will provide training and work with you for up to one year to learn the business. Once you have enough money "banked", it is then transferred into your own distributorship account. Apprenticeship programs are

great because they teach you how to generate customers and get trained even before you start your business. You now set yourself up for success from the start. Another way is to work with a distributor who will allow you to sell for her/him and put your commissions away until you have enough to start with the company.

## A Legacy for Your Family
This is where your MLM distributorship is considered a willable asset. If you grow your business to six figures and life is good, that's great, but what if something happens to you? Can you will your business to your wife/husband or a third party? Ensuring the continuation of your business so that your family does not have to worry is a very good feeling. Always ask if the venture that you are entering into is willable.

## Break Away
This is where the MLM company will actually "break away" one of the downlines from your organization if that downline is building at a stronger pace or if they start to out-earn you. The MLM company may then take the downline from your organization and give you a much smaller portion of their business than if it was still part of your downline. For example, if you normally receive 30% from the production of a specific downline, you may receive 4% after they break away. Hmmm... all that training and effort and now you are awarded with a pay cut. It kind of makes you wonder whether your upline will train you adequately, or inadequately in fear of eventually losing business? Not all MLM's are created equal, and not all MLM's have a "break-away" clause in their contract. Look for this prior to signing up.

## Training
It is critical to identify the level of training and support that you will receive from both the company and your immediate upline, as a new MLM distributor. Any training or assistance that the MLM company provides will be in writing and part of their business plan/model. This is a given. That said, do you expect the top dog to dedicate time and resources into training a new distributor that is seven levels down from him or her? Probably not. In this regard, it is best to set expectations with your sponsor (your upline, the one

that brought you into the business) as to the level of support that you may expect to receive from them. All training and support aside, it is up to YOU to come up to speed with what you need to in order to run a successful home-based MLM business. Read your manual. Work the program as instructed. Lucky for you, there is no reinventing of the wheel here.

## Bonuses

This is a question that many never ask: Are there bonuses and how are they paid? First, all companies have bonuses; however, many people do not understand how they are paid until they lose one. Get to know your bonus details! Many companies work by a point system. As your points grow higher, you may qualify for a bonus. In most cases from what I have seen, you need to reach your goal in a month's time. If you don't get the points or hit your goal in 30 days' time, you lose your bonus. Education is key. You need to learn the company's bonus rules. I have seen so many people work so hard to reach a goal, just to miss it by one point, and all they get is a pat on the back and an "attaboy, better luck next time." My advice is to look for bonuses that don't have a 30-day end time. Look for the longest end time; they are out there.

## Gifting Points

As you place orders that have a point structure you earn bonuses. Many companies have a "Business Volume" or the like attached to each product. This is good, and there are many companies that pay this way. Gifting points is a lot like sharing your volume. Ask if you can do this. Place an order and give the volume to the distributor at the bottom of your line. This way when the volume flows up… everyone can get a piece of the action. It's a really nice concept and helps to hold a team together. This will also aid in downline retention as it will decrease the percentage of people who quit.

## Horizontal vs. Vertical Marketing

Everything discussed up to this point has been characteristic of Horizontal marketing. Vertical marketing, also referred to as "Binary" marketing, provides an environment where everyone on a financial team has economic synergy. There are two organizations in vertical marketing where your team shares all commissions, and you get paid different percentages at various levels. What differentiates vertical from horizontal marketing is that only two organizations are required in vertical marketing, whereas six organizations is the average model in horizontal marketing. Why the number two? Because two is the smallest multiplier for the highest profits. One thing to know is that not all vertical organizations are considered MLM's (although most are). In vertical marketing you don't need to build as many teams. This makes life easier and provides the potential to make more money, while minimizing the (horizontal marketing) hassle of losing people in your downline. Be educated on the various percentages and how many levels down that you are compensated for. You want the highest percentage from your team for as many levels down as possible. Do your own research to ensure that the MLM company that you join is able to support its compensation model, or you might find yourself with an MLM that will go out of business.

MLM's work because they are backed up by a proven business model. The "trick", for lack of a better term, is to work the system as instructed. There is no reinventing the wheel. All said, not all MLM's are created equal. It is less a matter of a good versus bad MLM, than it is in finding the one that's right for you. You will get out of your business what you put into it.

As a mother of four children (three of them with special needs), the flexibility of a home-based MLM business has great appeal to me. It was very hard for me to go out into the work force and find a job that would allow me to care for my children, take them to doctor appointments, hospitals, or just take care of them without getting fired by a boss. Having a home-based business was the best option for me. I know a woman who had premature twins that weighed only one pound at birth. She spent months in the hospital with her two children with no worries as to where her next check was going to come from. She watched other moms cling to cell phones in futile attempts to convince their bosses to let them stay just a little longer. They had to leave their babies in the hands of doctors and nurses and hope that their children were still alive when they returned to the hospital from their jobs. Residual income is freedom to do what you want when you want with who you want. It's spending time with grandparents who are sick in the hospital while everyone else is stuck in an office. It's doing homework with your children at 3:00 in the afternoon or a family vacation that you can take whenever you want. You are your own boss, you eat when you want to eat, sleep until you are done, and tell yourself what you are worth.

One of my favorite questions that I get asked a lot is, "Do I have to sell?" The answer to this age-old (MLM) question is an emphatic "YES." Everyone is a salesperson. Whether you are selling a product or service, selling yourself to a potential employer or life partner, or selling your children on your beliefs, you are selling yourself each and every day of your life. When it comes to surviving your financial crisis, all options are on the table, and you shouldn't limit yourself or let any negative "I can't sell" thoughts creep into your psyche. Any business is work, and a home-based business is no exception. The hardest part is having the discipline to treat your home-based business like a business. Treat it like a million dollar business and it should pay you like one.

# Chapter 16

# Making Money from Home

## By Vivian C. Gaspar

Are you tired of crying, or just feeling like it, because there aren't any jobs to be had in your area, or 500 people are applying for each job opening? Do you think the phrase "work from home" is just a scam, or for anyone but you?

As someone who has found or created opportunities for myself to work from home for the last 25 years, I know that working from home is for anyone who can force themselves to be focused. The saying "necessity is the mother of invention" is very true. Basically, if you need money badly enough, you WILL do what it takes to make an opportunity work and ignore other issues which can make it difficult for the average person to work from home.

You do not need an extra bedroom to use as a home office. For the people who say that they do not have a separate home office they are simply using an excuse instead of finding a solution to that obstacle. For many years I used either a part of my small living room for my "office" or just worked at my dining room table. If you have children have them play in their rooms or watch TV in another room.

The other most common obstacle is, "I just can't concentrate. My cluttered house or dirty dishes are just calling to me." For that, my solution is to make both a weekly and a daily task list which will get you to a goal. Then be extremely focused on each task and clearly mark off each task as they are completed. Also, use a reward system for yourself. For example, after doing two important tasks "reward" yourself with a five minute break of a snack or TV or even checking your Facebook status.

Now that you have settled that you can be focused enough to work from home and where in your home you will work, what will you do?

The easiest way to work from home is telemarketing or cold calling. Anyone who has a phone and speaks clearly can train themselves to be an effective telemarketer. Forget the past negative experience you may have had with people pestering you at dinner time. Telemarketing is a very effective sales tool which generates billions of dollars in sales annually. I know you might be thinking that you do not want to be "one of THOSE bothersome people." However everyone who runs a small business needs more sales, and every salesperson regardless of who they work for or what they sell, would love qualified leads to call. The question to ask yourself is, "How badly do I need money and do I have the attitude that I am willing to do what it takes?" It has been estimated that 40% - 60% of a salesperson's time is spent generating leads, so all sales professionals would love to have qualified leads handed to them. By using leads which are provided to them, this makes any sales professional's income increase anywhere between 20-50% because they no longer need to take time to generate their own leads.

This is an occupation that you can easily do from home. Once you have proven yourself to be a reliable source you can easily get more work than you can handle and make anywhere from $8 to $20 per hour plus commission or bonus. Don't forget you now have tax savings as well by being able to write off your phone bill (or a portion thereof), a portion of your rent or mortgage, and other related expenses. This is now your business and you now set the rules and no longer have to worry about being laid off again. Also, you do not need to set up a company. You can be billed as 1099. Ask your CPA which is best for you.

OK, you are willing to give it a try, but how do you get customers to pay you? Well, don't think that by looking in your local paper or classified section on the Internet you will find a company local to you. That might happen, but it is not necessary for your clients to be close to you. After all, isn't the point of working from home that all you need is a phone? (A computer and Internet are preferable but not necessary.) You can work for anyone in the country. (I had a lady in Missouri doing telemarketing for me for several years. We never met and I live in New Jersey. She simply kept track of her hours and leads and I mailed her a check. I even paid a portion of her phone bill.)

You are still thinking — give me more details on how to find the clients. Think about what are the areas of the country where people tend to make more money, which means that the people and companies are used to paying more. As an example, you might live in Missouri or New Mexico where $7 or $8 an hour is a decent income, but the company or salesperson whom you solicit to give you business is in New Jersey, New York or Boston, where rates of pay are normally $10 to $12 an hour. This means you just earned more money for the same work just by soliciting business from areas which pay more than your area does.

Next, in the geographical target area of your choice, go online to Monster.com, Dice.com, or Careerbuilder.com, etc., and look for those companies hiring salespeople. Call or write offering telemarketing services to make their sales professionals more productive by giving them a head start with qualified leads. This might just be a new concept for them so they might tell you that is what their salesperson is responsible for. Don't let that deter you. Just keep trying. Remember, every company must sell something in order to stay in business. The sales section is normally the thickest section of any "classified" section as every company's income is brought in through sales. Remember, there are thousands of companies looking for sales help in the entire country.

By using persistence anyone can persuade a company looking for sales assistance to give a persistent telemarketer a try. One technique is to say that they can try your services free before committing. Think I am crazy? Think about it. If you are not making any money now, why not invest 5 hours of your time to prove to a company that it will pay off for them to hire you for a 20-30 hour a week commitment? If it does not work, are you really any worse off than you were before? Another technique is for you to place a services available ad on Craigslist or other similar websites. Through companies such as Vistaprint, you can even build your own website to advertise your services very inexpensively.

There is a section in this book which covers how to make effective telemarketing calls.

Other work from home service ideas are child care, performing errands for a fee, typing services or research assistance for college students, personal assistant services for busy sales professionals and for small business owners.

## Chapter 17

## LinkedIn: The Job Seeker's New Secret Weapon

## 7 Steps to get a job on LinkedIn

### By: Julbert J. Abraham

Right now, times are tough!! Unemployment rates are high and it is very challenging to find a decent job. A lot of people are struggling and living below the poverty line. To get a job, it is all about networking. You have to go out there. If you don't know anyone, you have to get to know folks because nowadays it's not what you know, it's who knows you. Therefore, anyone looking for work at this moment needs to think outside the box.

The power of thinking outside the box will allow you to use your imagination and separate yourself from the masses. This is where LinkedIn comes in play. Currently, there are over three hundred thirteen million professionals on LinkedIn; by the time you read this, it may be more, and this network gives you full access to one of the most powerful platforms in social media.

With LinkedIn you have access to decision makers, recruiters, job opportunities with your ideal company. The platform has allowed you to create a network of professionals that you can build a relationship with, then it can be used as a source for your job search.

In this chapter of the book, we are going to provide you with 7 steps on how to leverage LinkedIn to find your dream job. Please understand depending on when you read this book, these methods may change if there are changes on the platform; however, the concept will remain the same. In addition, you can start using these techniques immediately to build a network of professionals that can help you find the right opportunity for you.

**7 Steps to get a job on LinkedIn**

**1st Step** –Create a Strong LinkedIn Profile:

On LinkedIn, your profile is your face to the world. Your profile is your resume or your sales person to the world. That said, it is very important to have a great profile that represents you well. Your profile should include the following:

-Professional photo, preferably a head shot

-You need to have great content which includes your resume focusing on your past accomplishments and volunteering activities

- You should have a summary section that highlights your strength, what differentiates you from other candidates and how you can add value to any employers

-You should have at least 3-5 recommendations on your profile, from either your prior managers, peers, colleagues or partners. Recommendations are very important because it shows other people are speaking highly of you.

**2nd Step** – Build Your Network

LinkedIn has a great tool that shows you how you can connect with people who went to the same school as you, your classmates, friends, peers and administrators. Get to know your connections because your connection is your network on LinkedIn.

**3rd Step** – Make a list of 10-15 companies that you would like to work for; do research on them on LinkedIn. Find out where they are located, what kind of positions that are currently available and if you are actually qualified for these positions.

**4th Step** – LinkedIn gives you the ability to see who works at these companies. Find at least 3 people that work for each company that you know or are connected to someone within your current connections and ask your current connections for an introduction to these employees.

**5th Step** – Schedule an informational interview. After an introduction to these employees, your next step is to schedule an informational interview either over the phone or in person. The purpose of this informational interview is not to sell yourself to them or tell them that you need a job, it is relationship-building and learning more about the company and the work culture. It is your way of getting the "inside scoop."

**6th Step** – Once you build a relationship with the current employees, you want to reach out to them and ask them to introduce you to the person in their HR department or hiring managers.

**7th Step** – Once you get in contact with that key decision maker, build a relationship and when you are ready to apply for that position, reach out to him/her and express your intention and why you think you would be a great fit for that position.

**\*\*Preparation and developing relationships with the right people is key in our current economy.**

# Chapter 18

# The Real Estate Buying Guide

## By Frances Pepe

Yes, I want to buy a house! There are several key steps which are my easy to follow guide to buying a home. Your family home is the single largest investment you will ever make. Naturally, it is also where you and your family will build your life and make lifelong memories.

Please take a look at the few simple steps which I have outlined:

1) Planning and gathering knowledge is the key and the essential first step. Each person needs to evaluate their needs and wants. Knowing the marketplace and creating your buyer profile is essential to find your comfort zone. This may be a conflicting dilemma. Your buyer profile will help you to determine your niche...are you a first-time buyer, a move-up buyer or an empty nester? Evaluate your lifestyle and compile your "wish list." Your wants may be more aggressive than your needs. How much will it cost me? What is my credit score? How much are closing costs? What are closing costs? Who will give me a mortgage and where

do I get one? Do I really need a lawyer? Where do I want to live? Do I really want to commute? What is my time frame? What about my family? What costs are involved? Decisions and choices are all mine to make...what shall I do?

2) Knowing the key person in the marketplace that may be the essential piece in helping you sort through the plethora of information that will be bombarding you from all directions...the all-knowing family member, well-wishing friend, "I've been there" co-workers, and of course the all-inclusive factual Internet. At the ease of your fingertips is technology and information, very accessible and available on the Internet, which may give you facts. The key person that can answer your questions is an experienced and knowledgeable Real Estate professional that will offer and help you sort through the enormous amount of data to extract for you the essential information to answer your inquiries. Learn from their expertise, training and experience to capitalize on the key points to and shortcuts in the home-buying process. The more knowledgeable you are, the more definitive your goals. This is the key to a successful transaction. The selection of the "right" Realtor will enable you to establish a professional business relationship that will guide you through the myriad of homes, contract terms, financing options, current market conditions, negotiations, strategies for different situations/markets, inspection requirements, closing costs, legal ramifications and much more in the constantly changing marketplace. Your Realtor will keep you informed, updated and alerted to the constant changes in each step of the transaction process. Remember, recommendations are still the best way to get a Real Estate professional.

3) Financing and home-buying are intertwined. Purchasing a home requires a mortgage, unless you are fortunate to have cash, which does occur; however, most buyers prefer or need to obtain a mortgage. The difference between the purchase price of a home and the down payment is the mortgage amount. When determining how much you want to spend each month for a mortgage, you first must "qualify" and get an "approval." This is commonly known as getting "pre-qualified." Your income and debt ratio needs to be determined. The next crucial piece that is key in obtaining a mortgage is your credit score. Your mortgage professional will explain to you all you need to know about how credit scores are

primary factors in the rates and which type of mortgage you can obtain. What type of a mortgage you qualify for depends on your credit score, down payment, income and debt. These fundamental factors determine your qualification for a mortgage and the type of mortgage (Conventional, FHA, VA (for Veterans), USDA) that best suits you. All of this vital information is necessary to determine your purchase power. Your Mortgage Broker is the professional you will meet with and will get your financial paperwork in order to obtain your pre-approval. Once you have your letter of approval, you have purchase power to buy and are ready to begin your home search.

4) Your search begins...finding a home that suits your needs. What is most important to you? Go to your plan, your "wish list." Select the area or community of choice and target in on neighborhood, style of home, curb appeal, number of bedrooms / bathrooms, garage and yard size. So many choices, no two homes are alike and the housing market is constantly in flux. Honing in on the "perfect" home is a difficult task and finding the home with the amenities you want is exhausting and time consuming. After viewing several properties, you discover several are in your price range, and although they have the same number of bedrooms, one design may appeal to you more than another...the location, lot size, property tax, upgrades, kitchen features, flooring, exterior features, commuting distance, schools, shopping...there is a never-ending list of wants and needs. Finally, you need to consider your future needs several years from now, and the re-sale value if and when you want to sell. You must decide on a house that gives you an identity and value will be your home. Finally, you find a "perfect" house, and you know instantly that this is your home. It meets all of your requirements and expectations, and you fall in love; this is the one! This house is more than a shelter, it is where you live, relax, entertain, raise your family and work, it is your home! Now what?

5) The buying process begins after you select the home of your choice. The seller has placed their home on the market and has an established market price. The buyer now has to make an "offer." The buyer has to decide on the offer price. Extrapolating information from the current home sales, marker trends and affordability, the buyer with their pre-approval now has the purchase power to make an offer. Nothing is more complex,

variable, exciting, or personal than bargaining between the buyer and seller. The buyer makes an offer and the seller has three options: accept, reject or counter offer. This is where the expertise of the Realtor is evident in skillfully negotiating to a meeting of the minds. Once this is achieved and a purchase price is accepted, you now have a deal. A contract is signed by both the buyer and the seller, witnessed by the Realtor(s), and sent to their attorney(s) for review. The buyer needs to select an attorney and again, the experienced Realtor can guide the buyer to select a diligent Real Estate Attorney. The professionalism of the attorney is important to facilitate the easy progression through the legal closing process to home ownership. The attorney review period is usually three days not counting Saturday, Sunday or holidays; however, it may be extended by either attorney and/or may be canceled during the review period without any consequence to any party in the transaction. Upon the completion of the attorney review, the formal mortgage application is completed and the mortgage process begins.

6) The home inspection is the next step in the buying process. There are a number of inspections that are customary and common in residential real estate transactions, which include termite, structural, major systems (heating, plumbing, air conditioning are the major systems), radon, water, well and septic. Also, it may be necessary to have a survey to determine property boundaries as well as a property appraisal to establish value. It is important to note that if the appraisal value is less than the purchase price, it may be necessary to re-negotiate the sale price or put more money down to lower the mortgage amount. With the downturn of the real estate market and the decline in property values, appraisals are crucial to get a mortgage. It is necessary to "buy at the right price," especially in this marketplace. Again, your Realtor is the key in the real estate transaction and your best resource. All the pieces to the "buying puzzle process" must fit to accomplish finality to home ownership.

7) You are required to get three types of insurance when you purchase a home. The first type is homeowners insurance that is your necessary protection against loss of property from fire, theft, and provides liability coverage of your home, your most valuable asset. Essentially real estate insurance protects

owners in the event of a catastrophe; then it is the bargain of a lifetime. The second type of insurance is Title Insurance; that is a one-time fee charged at the closing that protects the owners in the event that the title to the property has a defect and/or is invalid. Coverage includes a "lenders" policy, which protects buyers up to the mortgage value of their property, and the "owners" coverage, which protects up to the purchase price (mortgage amount and down payment). The third type of insurance is flood and/or hurricane insurance, usually required in high-risk areas designated by the federal government. Home warranties are also available for new and existing homes. Usually the warranty policy is purchased by the seller for a one-year service contract that covers a breakdown or defects with major systems (plumbing, heating, pool pump, etc.) and is renewable for a fee. The time to purchase insurance and warranties for your home is at closing and needs to be discussed and agreed upon before closing. Again, your Realtor is your best resource and will assist you with every step in the purchase process.

8) The closing process is the "settlement" or "escrow" and varies in different parts of the country. Closing on your home brings together a variety of different parties who are part of the transaction process. You started with a plan, set your goals, selected your Realtor, searched for the prefect house, you made an offer, gave your down payment, received a mortgage, had your home inspections, got insurance, paid all the fees, and now you are signing the deed and getting the key to your new home. It is a set of checks and balances to insure that the history of ownership and chain of title has been checked and that the records do not contain errors, unrecorded claims, or flaws. At closing, transfer taxes are paid and other claims must also be settled (including legal fees, taxes, water and sewer charges, etc.). Settlement appears to be a brief process where all the necessary paperwork needed to complete the transaction is signed and culminates; this is usually at the buyer's attorney's office. The end result is the transfer of property from the seller to the buyer. The onerous and tedious buying process has ended and you have the key to your future, a new home, a new beginning!

9) After the closing, reality sets in. Go the post office and change your address.

Check on the status of your utilities required at your home (water, sewage, gas, electric, oil, cable, taxes). Next, prepare your budget and keep a minimum of three to six months' reserve for your expenses. You now have a big responsibility and need a cooling-off period with time to digest the turmoil of the hectic buying process and the fast-paced months that preceded this happy finality, home ownership!

10) Moving in...now you have to make it your own. First you clean and prepare to put all your personal possessions in their new places. Painting, decorating, new flooring, new furniture...pack up the old and unpack to the new. Many homeowners take photos and make a video record of their home and possessions for insurance purposes and keep the record in a safe and secure place. Your insurance company can give you guidelines of what to photograph and how to secure it. You may need an appraisal for expensive items (jewelry, paintings, collectibles, furs, etc.); check with your insurance company.  Maintain your fire, theft, and liability insurance and adjust coverage as the values of your property increase.  Lastly, owning a home is a serious responsibility. Remember it is a new tax deduction and most of all, enjoy your home and your new experience!

# Chapter 19

# Understanding Mortgages

## By Stephanie Banks

A woman said to me the other day, "UGH! Refinance! I don't want to go through THAT again!"

Given the fact that rates are now at historic lows, and she stood to save a substantial amount on her monthly mortgage payment, I should have been shocked. However, I understood her pain. Whether a refinance or a new purchase, many of us have had long, agonizing, drawn out, mortgage experiences.

There are many reasons an otherwise smooth process becomes stressful, and those reasons lie on both sides of the fence. In the next few pages, I hope to shed some light on residential mortgages and the lending process, hopefully enabling you to make informed decisions in meeting your financing goals.

**In The Beginning**
When shopping for a mortgage, many of us start out by doing

some research online, filling out short forms, looking for the best rates that will save us the most money. We may get calls from various mortgage companies, or we may venture out to our neighborhood lender.

No matter whom you do business with – a mortgage banker or a mortgage broker – you should only work with a Licensed Mortgage Professional.

Back in the early 2000's when home values were ridiculously off the charts, people were coming out of the woodwork to become "loan officers" and take advantage of the increased income possibilities. Unfortunately, many were also taking advantage of the borrower. People with no prior financial or sales experience were working in this industry because borrowers were suddenly equity rich on paper. It didn't take a rocket scientist to convince that borrower to refinance their precious home and take cash out for other things (usually to pay off debt that was re-accumulated shortly afterward). To add insult to injury, more often than not, that well-meaning borrower was put into a loan that they didn't qualify for, or should not have been in, such as: Pay Option Arms for people who wanted to stay in their homes long-term, No Documentation loans, No Down Payment or 100% financing for people whose credit was short of stellar. The result has been disastrous. Let me pause for a moment and make it clear that obviously not all mortgage people were unscrupulous. The good ones back then are the best ones now – professional, caring and responsible individuals who have built relationships with their clients. So why did all those nice borrowers (maybe you!) get swept up in the craziness? Well, because you trusted us. And why shouldn't you? We are the experts in home financing. You wouldn't come to us with a sore throat, any more than you would go to your doctor for your home loan. Unfortunately, the mortgage industry had their share of quacks as well, but unlike the medical and other professions, we were not required to be licensed, there was virtually no standard nor regulation, and many mortgage companies turned a blind eye toward compliance laws because no one was looking over their shoulder.

**Problem Solved**
In July of 2008, the Office of the Comptroller of the Currency, Board of Governors of the Federal Reserve System, Federal Deposit Insurance Corporation, Office of Thrift Supervision, Farm Credit Administration, and National Credit Union Administration ("the agencies") published the final rules for implementing the federal registration requirements of the Secure and Fair Enforcement of Mortgage Licensing Act of 2008 (S.A.F.E. ACT), otherwise known as Public Law 110-289, Title V.

All mortgage bankers, mortgage brokers and individual mortgage originators were required to be licensed by the National Mortgage Licensing System and Registry in order to continue working in the industry. It requires educational courses, passing the federal licensing exam, extensive background checks including fingerprinting on the federal and state level, as well as proving financial responsibility. Additionally, each state that we originate loans in requires coursework in that state's mortgage and compliance laws and passing the state licensing exam.

So how do you know if the loan officer you are doing business with is licensed?

Licensed companies and individuals are given a unique identifying number. It is required to appear on all business cards and other forms of advertising. If you are doing business with someone who cannot provide a licensing number that is attached to THEIR name, not their company's name, you should probably turn on your heels and scoot. The National Mortgage Licensing System and Registry (NMLS) has a website, www.nmlsconsumeraccess.com, with information on all licensed and registered individuals and companies nationwide. To be fair, when looking someone up by name, make sure to have their full name, including middle initial or spelling out their middle name if necessary. Loan officers who are employed by federally chartered banks, savings and loans, or credit unions do not have to be licensed, but are still registered, as are their respective institutions, with the NMLS. You will find their names on the registry as well.

## Mortgage Banker vs. Broker vs. Your Hometown Bank

Now that you're ready to find that perfect mortgage, what type of mortgage professional will best suit your needs?

Mortgage banks are state licensed, originate loans directly to the borrower, and fund loans with their own capital or warehouse line of credit. The advantages to working with a mortgage banker are many. In addition to offering competitive rates, they basically have control over the total lending environment. In other words, origination, processing and underwriting are done "in house," allowing for a more personal touch to your particular scenario. The communication between all parties involved has virtually 0 degrees of separation, resulting in an efficient and quick delivery of the loan approval and clear to close.

Mortgage bankers lend their own product line, which some may see as a limiting disadvantage. However, many mortgage bankers have a varied product line and are highly competitive in the market. Costs should be lower when working with a mortgage banker as well because there are no "middleman" fees.

A mortgage broker is an intermediary who puts the borrower together with the lender (mortgage banker). Their product line can be as varied as the lenders they do business with, enabling them to accommodate many lending needs. However, as the middle person they are working depending upon processors and underwriters who are employees of the various lenders, not their co-workers. Although this works, those same processors, underwriters and closers are also working on files from their in-house loan officers. Your file is from the broker who is calling in.

Additionally, mortgage brokers cannot lock your rate or grant you a pre-approval. All decisions come directly from the lender they are submitting your application to. By the nature of the process, closing times can be extensive as well, between 45-60 days.

Your neighborhood savings and loan may already have a relationship with you if you are an account holder, although it's not a prerequisite for a loan. However, this is not their primary business and their mortgage products may not be as competitive.

In most instances, even with the large household name banks, your application is taken at the branch level by a customer service representative. With all respect due to them, they are not usually privy to lending guidelines. Your application is then submitted to a corporate mortgage department and out of the hands of the original person who took your information. Lending guidelines can be stricter as well, so unless you are the perfect borrower, don't expect to be offered a chair and a cup of coffee, much less a mortgage.

The best of both worlds is the mortgage banker who has an extensive product line AND can broker out any special situations that his/her product guidelines don't normally accommodate.

**What's Your Rate?**
My intention was to segue into "Types of Mortgages" at this point in the chapter, but since this is the question everyone asks first, it pulled rank. First of all, when it comes to buying a home or refinancing, you should never shop for a mortgage based simply on advertised lowest interest rate quotes. Today's consumer needs good advice from an experienced, educated mortgage professional who has the consumer's best interest in mind.

This means BEWARE of anyone who quotes you an interest rate over the phone or the Internet without asking anything about you, your family, your finances or your lifestyle. Besides market conditions, your mortgage rate is based on a long list of criteria that are unique to your individual financial situation.

Look at the list below of 15 different criteria that affect your mortgage rate. How can anyone quote you an interest rate you can trust without a thorough knowledge of your unique financial situation?

1. Amount of Mortgage
2. LTV ( loan to value ratio) based on value of your property
3. Type of Property - primary residence? is it an investment, do you collect rent, is it a townhome or condo, is the condo warrantable or not? do you pay association fees?
4. DTI (debt to income ratio)

5. Type of Employment and Income (are you a W-2 employee, 1099, or self-employed, are you retired, collecting SS and a pension, early retirement with just a pension? Are you on disability – permanent or temporary, are you on family leave, returning to the same job, are you a union worker with sporadic employment, are you on temporary layoff?)
6. Type of Loan – Conventional or FHA, USDA, VA? Is it an adjustable?
7. Cash-out or a rate and term refinance?
8. Do you escrow your taxes and insurance?
9. What is your credit score?
10. If a purchase – how much of a down payment do you have?
11. Is any of your down payment a gift from a family member?
12. What kind of assets do you have and can you document them?
13. Length of Loan – 30yr, 20, 15, 10?
14. Co–borrower (all of the above)?
15. Will you pay points to buy down your rate?

**What Causes Interest Rate Movement**
The Federal Reserve constantly evaluates the US economy and, when necessary, takes steps to address inflationary concerns and avoid economic recession or depression. The mass media, in turn, reacts by providing a wide range of opinions and interpretations of the Fed's monetary policy. This can make it very difficult for consumers to decipher how such actions will influence interest rates in general, and mortgages in particular.

Although actions of the Federal Reserve can have a direct impact on the Prime rate, mortgage interest rates are dictated by the trading of mortgage-backed securities, which are similar to bonds and trade on a daily basis. This means that the real dynamic at the heart of interest rate movement is the competitive relationship between stocks and bonds.

Stocks, bonds, and mortgage-backed securities compete for the same investment dollars on a daily basis. There is literally only so much money to be invested. When the Federal Reserve feels that interest rates need to be decreased in an effort to stimulate the economy, this reduction in rates can often cause a stock market rally. When the market becomes bullish, the money to invest in stocks comes from the selling off of other investments, including mortgage-backed securities.

Unfortunately, when mortgage-backed securities are sold off to fuel stock market rallies, this causes interest rates to go up, not down.

Historically, there have been many instances where the Federal Reserve has increased interest rates, arousing fears that corporate profit margins would be affected. This resulted in stocks being sold off, leading money managers to search for a place to invest their newly liquidated assets until the next market rally. One such safe haven has been mortgage-backed securities, which cause mortgage rates to drop.

The daily ebb and flow of money is what matters most when it comes to the movement of mortgage interest rates. I make it a point to continuously monitor interest rates for my clients and advise them of opportunities to manage their mortgage debt at a better rate. This is the foundation of my business model as a trusted advisor.

**What type of mortgage is best for me?**
Finding a mortgage that's right for you should be easy. However, there are often many different programs to choose from, as well as a myriad of ways to structure your loan in terms of the amount financed, term, payment, rate, closing costs and so forth.

Because there are so many options available, it's important to seek advice from an experienced mortgage professional who is looking out for your interests. The first step in determining which program is right for you is to ask yourself the important questions listed below. These questions can also help you confirm that you've chosen the right mortgage professional as well, because he or she should be asking you the same questions before trying to put any mortgage in place:

- How long do you anticipate living in your home?

- Do you expect any changes over the next few years, such as expanding your family or having children go off to college or even move away?
- Do you expect any changes in income such as promotions, downsizing, retirement, inheritance, or pensions?
- Are you expecting a change with regard to your investments?
- When it comes to investment strategies, are you conservative, aggressive, or somewhere in between?

These questions are important in that different loan programs will offer specific benefits that will appeal to borrowers at different stages of life. What one homeowner might find desirable might cause another to reach for the antacids!

Your mortgage professional should give you a complete picture of exactly how much your mortgage will cost over the period of time you anticipate having the loan. This is the single most important factor you should consider when shopping for a mortgage. Not only does this data illustrate the bigger picture of your financial goals, it allows for adjustments should things change a little sooner than expected. A good timeframe for this projection is anywhere from three, five, or even up to seven years.

## Types of Mortgages

Whether a refinance or a new purchase, there are many types of mortgage products to choose from, each having advantages and disadvantages depending on your situation. Because this is the largest investment most people make, it is important that you do some research and gain some understanding as to what is best for you. Your mortgage professional, in my opinion, is OBLIGATED to educate you and make sure you understand the mortgage product they are qualifying you for and why. Don't forget the old adage, "there is no such thing as a stupid question." Ask, ask, ask, until you are comfortable.

## Fixed Rate Mortgages

30 year Fixed Rate Mortgages - this is the one most folks are looking for. It is also the mortgage product that makes the most sense if you plan to own your home for more than five years. The

advantages are the obvious protection against inflation – if rates go up, yours won't. You always know what your interest is going to be, regardless of what's happening in the market, making it a low risk mortgage. Additionally, it allows you to budget and plan for other long term financial goals because you know what your payment will be for the life of the loan.

Another factor to consider with a fixed rate mortgage is that even though the rate stays the same, if your taxes or homeowners insurance increase, obviously so will your payment. Also, if mortgage rates go down, the only way to take advantage of a lower payment would be to refinance. The most important factor, however, is that 30 year fixed rates are traditionally higher than other loan products such as adjustable rate mortgages. Therefore you may not be able to qualify for as large a loan amount.

Fixed rate mortgages are available as 40, 30, 25, 20, 15, and 10 year loans. It is important to understand that even though the rates may be lower on a shorter term mortgage, the payment is usually higher because you are financing over a shorter period of time. This may sound pretty obvious, but you would be surprised how many people tell me they are looking for a lower rate, lower payments AND to shorten the term of the mortgage. Not usually happening. As an example:

The payment on a $200,000 mortgage at 5.00% for 30 years would be $1073.64.

The payment on a $200,000 mortgage at 4.50% for 15 years would be $1529.99.

In order for the 15 year payment to be lower than the borrower's current 30, he would have to currently be paying a rate of 8.5% or higher.

A quick word about 40 year loans – yes, the payments are lower, enabling you to qualify for a larger loan. After all, you are spreading those payments out over an extra 10 years. However, not only is the interest rate usually a bit higher, you are also paying that interest over an additional 10 years, and paying toward principal at a much slower pace. Some 40 year programs amortize over a full 40 years; however, some programs have a balloon payment at the end of 30 years.

**Hybrid Adjustable** – (sometimes referred to as Short-Term Fixed Rate mortgages, or Hybrids) come in numerous varieties; the 3, 5, 7, and 10-Year Fixed. These are all 30-year loans that carry a fixed rate for a set number of years, and then roll over to an Adjustable Rate Mortgage.

For example, in a 7-Year Fixed Rate scenario, the rate would be fixed the first seven years, and the loan becomes an Adjustable for the remaining 23 years. The main advantage of these hybrid programs is typically they have a slightly lower interest rate then a 30 year fixed.

These types of loans often work well for people who do not plan on being in their home for an extended period of time, such as first time home buyers. The most important question to ask when going into an Intermediate Fixed Mortgage is how long will the borrower need the money?

If the borrower intends to sell the home in four to five years, then a 5-Year Fixed loan offers stability and a lower interest rate for the time that money is needed. However, in this example it may not be wise to pay points up front to obtain a lower interest rate, because the likelihood of recuperating the cost of those points would be diminished because of the short time in the loan.

Please be aware that these are Adjustable Mortgages. I recently spoke to a gentleman who was working with another lender. He insisted that he was getting a 5 year fixed mortgage. The problem here was that it was presented to him by the loan officer in such a way that he believed his loan to be akin to a 30 year traditional fixed rate loan. He had no idea it was an adjustable mortgage, and never would have agreed to that type of financing. He was told that after 5 years the rate would go up. He assumed that it would then stay at the new rate. It really didn't matter to him because he was convinced that he would be out of the house in five years anyway. However, the issue here is that he really didn't know the product.

What if something in his life changed that prevented him from selling his home in 5 years, the rate started to adjust up (it can go down) and he was unable to refinance? Overall, this may have been the right product for his situation, but it wasn't presented to him truthfully and therefore prevented him from making an informed decision.

**How Adjustable Rate Mortgages Work**
During the last decade, Adjustable Rate Mortgages (ARMs) have increased in popularity among consumers. According to national studies, few homeowners (especially first-time buyers) remain in their homes for more than seven years. In this case, it often makes sense to get an adjustable rate mortgage with a lower rate, especially one with a 5-year or 7-year fixed portion, since they won't have the loan long enough to be concerned about rate fluctuation.

Adjustable Rate Mortgages have three main features: Margin, Index, and Caps. The Margin is the fixed portion of the adjustable rate. It remains the same for the duration of the loan. The Index is the variable portion. This is what makes an ARM adjustable. Margin + Index = Interest Rate.

It's important to understand that there are many different indices: The 11th District Cost of Funds (COFI), the Monthly Treasury Average (MTA), The One Year Treasury Bill, the Six Month Libor, etc. Each index has its own strengths and weaknesses; some are slow moving, others are more aggressive.

The third and final component of Adjustable Rate Mortgages is Caps. Caps limit how much the rate can fluctuate over time. Annual Caps limit changes to the annual rate, whereas Life Caps provide a worst case scenario over the life of the loan.

**FHA Loans** – differ from typical loans in that they are insured by the Federal Housing Administration, which is a part of the Department of Housing and Urban Development (HUD). Because this insurance reduces the lender's risk on the loan, lenders have greater flexibility with regard to approving loans. For example, FHA loans are not as restrictive with minimum credit scores, so a client may be able to obtain a loan despite having had credit problems or even a bankruptcy in the past. Alternatively, if a consumer does not have a significant traditional credit history, it may still be possible to obtain financing by documenting payment histories on items such as rent and utilities. Not all lenders accept these alternate forms of credit, so ask your mortgage consultant for additional clarification.

FHA loans also provide added flexibility when it comes to closing costs and the down payment. Many of the closing costs can be incorporated into the loan, and a down payment of as little as 3.5% of the purchase price is required, or if a refinance, the minimum equity required. Additionally, in the case of a purchase, the down payment may be obtained as a gift from a family member or through a down-payment assistance program.

**The Advantages of FHA Loans**
In many regions of the US, FHA loans have only recently come back into vogue, so a lot of real estate agents and mortgage originators aren't familiar with this great resource. The following are a just a few of the recent changes that have made FHA loans a more attractive option again for some consumers looking to buy a new home or refinance an existing one:

1. Congress passed the Stimulus Act of 2008. During the recent housing boom, home values surpassed FHA loan limits in many regions of the US. The recent enactment of this important legislation, however, increased FHA loan limits up to $729,500 in many high-cost regions of the US through the end of the year. FHA loan limits vary by county, so ask your mortgage professional for loan limits in your area.

2. The FHA changed its appraisal and fee negotiating guidelines. In the past, many sellers steered clear of FHA loans because the appraisals were too strict and certain fees were nonnegotiable. The FHA has greatly loosened these guidelines to make it easier for both buyers and sellers.

3. FHA loans are much cheaper now. Because FHA loans are federally insured, they tend to trade at a higher premium in

the secondary market. This means lenders can often charge a lower rate.

4. FHA loans are typically not as credit-score restrictive. Borrowers usually can have a lower score than with other products and still qualify for a good rate.

5. FHA loans require as little as 3.5% down, and allow

   a. Sellers to contribute up to 6% of the buyer's purchase price to close

   b. In a refinance, homeowners to take cash out up to 85% of the home's value; and

   c. Homeowners to consolidate first and seasoned second mortgages up to 97.75% of the home's value.

   FHA loans also require an upfront mortgage insurance premium as well as a monthly premium. Because of the many advantages of FHA loans, especially for borrowers who would otherwise not qualify for a conventional mortgage, the benefits far outweigh this additional cost which can usually be recouped in a few years via the savings from the lower interest rate.

## A Word About Points and When Should You Pay Them

Points are up-front fees paid by the borrower to obtain a better interest rate on a loan, essentially "buying down" the rate. One point equals one percent of the loan amount. While a lower interest rate may result in a lower monthly payment, it is important to consider how long you intend to be in the loan and to compare current interest rates to historical market trends. This will help you to determine whether paying points is a worthwhile investment.

As an example, if you take out a $300,000 mortgage and decide to pay one point in order to lower your interest rate, this would translate into an up-front cost of $3,000. Just to keep it simple, we'll assume that paying this one point will save you $50 a month. This means it will take you 60 months to recoup the cost of that point. If you decide to refinance or sell the home before the 60-month mark, your money is lost – not to mention the opportunity cost of not having this money invested elsewhere. In this scenario, you would only benefit financially from paying points if you were to remain in the home for no less than 60 months.

It's also important to remember that interest rates run in cycles. When rates are at historical lows, it makes more sense to pay points if you plan to live in the home for an extended period of time. If it's unlikely that rates will go down in the near future, then there will be no need to refinance.

When interest rates are high, however, there is a strong likelihood that they will come down again before too long. Therefore, this is not a good time to pay points. The chances of refinancing in the near future are extremely high, and you will likely not be in the loan long enough to recoup the up-front cost of the points.

Tax deductibility is another thing to consider when choosing whether or not to pay points. For new purchases, interest from both points paid and your mortgage are tax deductible up front. For refinances, however, points are not deductible up front. Instead
the deductions are spread out over the term of the loan (unless the entire loan is paid off early), making points more costly in comparison.

**Credit Scoring**
There are five factors that comprise the credit score. They are listed below in order of importance, just as an underwriter would look at the score:

- Payment History: 35% impact. Paying debt on time and in full has a positive impact. Late payments, judgments and charge-offs have a negative impact. Missing a high payment has a more severe impact than missing a low payment. Delinquencies that have occurred in the last two years carry more weight than older items.

- Outstanding Credit Balances: 30% impact. This factor marks the ratio between the outstanding balance and available credit. Ideally, the consumer should make an effort to keep balances as close to zero as possible, and definitely below 30% of the available credit limit when trying to purchase a home.

- Credit History: 15% impact. This marks the length of time since a particular credit line was established. A seasoned borrower is stronger in this area.

- Type of Credit: 10% impact. A mix of auto loans, credit cards, and mortgages is more positive than a concentration of debt from credit cards only.

- Inquiries: 10% impact. This quantifies the number of inquiries that have been made on a consumer's credit history within a six-month period. Each hard inquiry can cost from 2 to 50 points on a credit score, but the maximum number of inquiries that will reduce the score is 10. In other words, 11 or more inquiries in a six-month period will have no further impact on the borrower's credit score.

Remember, a computer that's not taking any personal factors into consideration calculates these scores. When a credit report is generated, it is simply today's snapshot of your credit profile. This can fluctuate dramatically within the course of a week, depending on your activities. You should be aware that when you enter into the loan process, know that it's not in your best interest to go out on a shopping spree. Please make sure you are not creating a negative impact on your score while your lender is reviewing your file.

When a lender runs your credit, they are compiling a tri-merge credit report. This provides scores from the three credit bureaus, Experian®, TransUnion®, and Equifax. The lender should be provided with this rounded profile because these three scoring systems can vary in their results. The lender is going to look at the middle score and throw out the other two. In many cases, this works to the borrower's advantage.

## What Constitutes Closing Costs?

Second to the popular question, "what are your rates?" is "what are your closing costs?" Closing costs are expenses that cover fees associated with the transfer of property ownership, fees paid to state and local governments, and the costs of obtaining a mortgage loan. In the case of a new purchase, some of these fees are negotiable, and could be paid by either the buyer or the seller. In all lending situations some costs are one-time fees (non-recurring closing costs, such as title search, termite inspection, appraisal, etc.), while other fees such as homeowners insurance or property taxes are things you will expect to continue to pay on a regular basis as a homeowner.

When looking at closing costs, especially in the case of a refinance, usually the largest portion of money is appropriated for escrows, with the exception of points if you are paying them. If the lender is disclosing properly, these numbers should be relatively the same no matter who you are doing business with. Many times a lender will disclose six months' taxes and insurance on the initial Good Faith Estimate, knowing that on the final Settlement Statement the number may be reduced to three or four months. Conventional wisdom says it's better to over disclose and have your numbers come down in the end as opposed to under disclosing. Unfortunately, many loan originators will under disclose because they are keenly aware of most borrowers' apprehension of closing costs. As an example, they will disclose two months' taxes and two months' homeowners insurance to be held in escrow. Another "trick" is the per diem interest. This interest is calculated based on your new rate and the day of the month you close. Many loan officers will calculate at one day as opposed to, say, 15 days. These two examples will heavily impact the bottom line. It will make their closing cost appear very low and cause the borrower to stop talking to anyone who is higher. Obviously, when the borrower gets to the closing table, they are in for a big surprise.

As part of the loan selection process, your mortgage consultant should be giving you some idea of how much money you should have in reserve to cover your end of these costs if you are not rolling it into the mortgage. The Real Estate Settlement Procedures Act (RESPA) requires the lender to provide you with a Good Faith Estimate within three days of the submission of your loan application.

RESPA also states that as a home buyer, you have the legal right to request a copy of the HUD-1 Settlement Statement 24 hours before your closing is scheduled. The HUD-1 clearly defines all closing costs, including those that are to be paid by the buyer and the seller. It's a good idea to have both of these forms before your closing so you can compare the estimated costs to the actual costs before you finalize your transaction.

## Five Reasons to Refinance Your Mortgage

There is an old adage in the mortgage business that states that if you can improve your interest rate by at least one to two percentage points, then it is a good time to refinance. While that may work as a general rule of thumb, the truth is that there are many reasons to refinance. Here are a few:

### Lower your interest rate.
Securing a lower interest rate is one of the top reasons for refinancing. This can make a big difference in your monthly out-of-pocket costs for housing and save money on financing fees.

### Build equity faster.
If you are in a position to make higher monthly payments due to an increase in salary or other good fortune, you may want to switch from a 30-year loan program into a 15- or 20-year loan structure. This enables you to build equity faster and save a tremendous amount of money on financing fees.

### Change your loan program.
Some homeowners who start out in an Adjustable Rate Mortgage (ARM) find that they would like to switch to the stability of a Fixed Rate mortgage at some point. An ARM may have been the most attractive rate and loan package when you first financed your

home, but we can provide you with loan comparison charts to find out if you can save money with another type of loan program that might work better for you right now.

**Credit score has improved.**
If your credit score has improved as a result of making your mortgage payments on time and in full, you may be in a position to take advantage of your improved credit standing. We can review your current credit score, the terms of your existing mortgage, and review options for other loan programs that could not only reduce your monthly payment, but also save you money on interest fees paid over the life of the loan.

**Use the equity you have established.**
A cash-out refinance allows you to tap into the equity you have built up in your home. You may want to pay off revolving credit card accounts, send a child to college, or use the money for home improvements or personal expenses.

Regardless of your reasons for wanting to refinance your existing mortgage, my team and I are interested in helping you make a decision that works best for you.

When shopping for a mortgage, you should always evaluate your choices carefully and consider how they will fit in with your long-term financial plan.

As always, I'd be happy to answer any questions and help calculate any scenarios that can help you determine what you can afford or save in today's market. Together, we'll find the program that's best for you! Just call or email me today.

# Chapter 20

# Mortgage Modification: Use it to Save Your Home and Sanity

## By Vivian C. Gaspar & V. James Castiglia, Esq.

Foreclosure and Short Sale are terms that unfortunately have become all too commonplace recently. Often they are thought to be the only road to go down for those who have been affected by the economy because of a recent drop in income, a life change or are just unable to refinance due to the changes in the banking guidelines. A mortgage modification is restructuring (making changes to) the terms of your existing mortgage.

It is not a refinance, and there are no closing costs. However, there might be minor fees which your lender may charge. The main way to be certain they are modifying your mortgage vs. refinancing is that modification fees will never include recollection of your property taxes for escrow.

Mortgage modification can get existing mortgages to an affordable rate and, in some cases, get a relief period of between two to five years and a payment rate of between 2% to 4%. Also, forbearances are possible, which can vary from lender to lender. Ask your lender what they can offer. The average person has an interest rate of 6%. Imagine you would now pay half to a third of that payment to help them stay in their homes and prevent the ever increasing American ghost town.

The HAMP, or Home Affordability Mortgage Protection Act, also known as the "making home affordable" act, was enacted in March 2009. The basic benefit is to bring the mortgage payment down to 31% mortgage debt to income ratio or an effective 2% mortgage interest rate for 60 months with the rate increasing by 1% a year until it is back to your current interest rate. There are several caveats to this program, however; the loan amount cannot exceed $729,000 for a single family, the property must be owner-occupied and the home owner cannot be past 12 months in arrears with payments. Also, it is very important that the borrower's monthly income needs to be in a very specific ratio of 3x the proposed modified payment including property taxes, homeowners hazard insurance and any associated association dues. The reason is that if your gross household income is less than 3x that, the idea is you cannot even afford a modified payment over time, and if your income exceeds that 3x calculation, then lenders deem you should be able to afford your mortgage payment. They also will take into account your net income and your expenses. However, there are some points of logic that will apply, such as: have you taken vacations or purchased non-necessity large ticket items when you fell behind in your mortgage payments, or do you have multiple car payments and cannot pay your mortgage? (They will say get a used car without car payments so you can save on monthly expenses.) Also, small independent lenders can refuse to modify at all.

## Mortgage Modification - Frequently Asked Questions

### Question #1:
Are my credit score, current home value, or available equity factors for qualification?

### Answer #1:
Short Answer: No.

Long Answer: While these are not factors for qualification, significant equity in a home may impact negotiation or qualification.

**Question #2:**
Who is a good candidate for a mortgage modification?

**Answer #2:**
Any homeowner who is having a hardship. Good examples include:

    a) Homeowners who have had an ARM reset higher; experienced a job loss or loss of 2nd income; experienced a divorce; caring for an elderly parent; experienced a sickness or incurred medical expenses; other hardship where loss of income or increased expenses have occurred.

    b) Business owners whose personal income has decreased as a result of a drop in business revenues.

**Question #3:**
Does a mortgage modification affect my credit score?

**Answer #3:**
Yes; however, to what degree is not an exact answer. Don't forget your credit score is comprised of several factors such as the number of creditors you have open and for how long, any judgments or liens, also ratio of available and used credit per credit card are just a few examples of how your total credit score is comprised and on what factors your credit history is judged.

**Question #4:**
What information is needed in order to have my mortgage modified?

**Answer #4:**
    1. Information on your current mortgage, including: principal amount; interest rate; mortgage term; monthly payment (with & without escrows); annual taxes; mortgage lender; loan origination date; is homeowners insurance escrowed?;

explanation of hardship. Provide this information for each mortgage note.

2. Supporting documentation, including: last year's tax return; last four pay-stubs or unemployment stubs; last four bank statements; current mortgage statement.

**Question #5:**
What are your recent success stories?

**Answer #5:**
See below – 13 recent successes:

Case #1:
Customer's monthly mortgage payment was reduced by 57% for a two year period. The money saved was completely forgiven by the bank, and not owed on the back end of the mortgage.

Case #2:
Customer's interest rate went from 10% to 3.9% for a five year period (they did not have to refinance). The money saved was completely forgiven by the bank, and not owed on the back end of the mortgage.

Case #3:
Customer did not pay the mortgage for two years and owed $52,000 in arrears to the bank (sheriff's sale was imminent). Our attorney stopped the sheriff's sale, and negotiated a 90% forgiveness of arrears, in addition to an affordable monthly payment. Let's be more clear on this: in the end, the customer only had to pay $5,200.00 of the original $52,000.00, plus the negotiated affordable mortgage payment.

Case #4:
Customer's monthly mortgage payment went from $3,500 a month to $1,900 a month.

Case #5:
Customer's monthly mortgage payment went from $4,800 a month to $3,200 a month.

Case #6:
Customer's monthly mortgage payment went from $2,000 a month to $1,300 a month.

Case #7:
Customer's monthly mortgage payment went from $6,188 a month to $2,828 a month.

Case #8:
Customer's monthly mortgage payment went from $3,600 a month to $2,117 a month.

Case #9:
For a second Mortgage:
Customer's monthly mortgage payment went from $611 a month to $298 a month.

Case #10:
Customer's monthly mortgage payment went from $4,055 a month to $2,943 a month.

Case #12:
Customer's monthly mortgage payment went from $2,548 a month to $1,700 a month during trial period, then to $1,348 for permanent modification.

Case #13:
Second Mortgage: Offer In Compromise:
$64,000 owed was negotiated to be completely settled for $15,000 cash lump sum. (Lump sum can be borrowed from any source of customer's choice.)

Again, it is really important to realize that the "business" of mortgage modification is constantly changing and what the individual banks/lenders are willing to actually do to assist the homeowner is also ever changing. The federal government has stepped in; however, their regulations set forth in the "making home affordable" guidelines have been followed to varying degrees by different lenders. The key is to be persistent, not take the first denial as the final word, and research the guidelines of your state's department of banking as to who is legally allowed to assist with mortgage modification if you choose to go that route. If you are going to do the modification effort without assistance, then do your due diligence and carefully research the guidelines for the "making home affordable" modification program, making sure you follow the guidelines on how they want the information presented and be outspoken with working with your lender on what the guidelines state. Do not just settle for their possibly inferior in-house programs which are likely to have less of a reduction of payment for less time. Read the modification agreement very carefully before signing, and if possible, have it reviewed by an experienced real estate attorney. Remember, most modifications have trial payments that cannot be late by even one day or they can deny you for the permanent, long-term modification. Also, equally important, you may constantly and continually be under scrutiny during the trial period until the final modification is signed by both parties, you the borrower, and the lender.

## Chapter 21

# Understanding the Foreclosure Process: Why Short-Sale vs. Foreclosure?

**By Vivian C. Gaspar & V. James Castiglia, Esq.**

The housing crisis, which started in 2007, was attributed to many factors. The consequences included the closing of thousands of mortgage banks of all sizes (among them the U.S.'s largest subprime lender, New Century, which had closed over $50 billion in mortgage loans just the prior year). Many experts have pointed the blame at the loose lending practices of the very banks which closed and fell victim to the domino effect of their own over-flexible lending guidelines. The bottom line is, now what happens to the individual homeowners who got caught up in this mortgage mess in one way or another?

Education is and should be the homeowner's primary tool in understanding not just their rights and obligations, but their options as what to do and what not to do.

The first thing that a homeowner should NOT do is give up too easily or move out of their home prematurely when they fall behind in payments. In the news there have been reports of homeowners putting the keys to their homes into envelopes, mailing them to their mortgage lender, and moving out of the home. The media has coined the term "jingle envelopes" for this very action. In some cases the homeowner did this as an act of defiance or to make a statement. More troubling is the homeowner who genuinely believes that by mailing back the keys of their home to their mortgage bank they are released from their mortgage obligation. This is completely false! The only way to release the homeowner of any further obligation on the mortgage of that home is by 1) paying it off in full, 2) obtaining a signed short sale agreement from the lender authorizing a short payoff or 3) having a foreclosure lawsuit finalized by the lender against the borrower.

A foreclosure is the type of judgment that is filed against a borrower by the lending mortgage bank due to lack of payments by the homeowner/borrower. The enforcement action is to take legal ownership of the home away from the homeowner and transfer it to the lender. This happens with a sheriff's sale which comes at the end of the foreclosure process. The homeowner can be evicted from the property only after this process. This process does vary from state to state since this is a legal action on the state, not the federal, level. In some states, the homeowner can be more than 24 months (two years) in arrears before getting to the point of a sheriff's sale, while in other states a sheriff's sale action can come in as little as five months of non-payment of the mortgage. It is very important that if you fall behind in your mortgage payment that you check with your county sheriff's department to see how long the process takes in your state. Also, it is important to understand what happens after the sheriff's sale. Does the home owner need to vacate the property the same day? In some cases, believe it or not, you can actually pay rent to the very lender which foreclosed upon you to actually continue to reside in the home (you once owned) as a paying tenant!

If you want to move on with your life and move out of the home (perhaps the lender will not rent to you, or you owe much more than the value of the home), you need to understand the differences and when and why to do a short sale vs. allowing your home to be foreclosed upon. Following are the alternatives to a foreclosure/sheriff's sale:

**Traditional Sale** – you sell your home with or without the aid of a Realtor, you sell the home for more than you owe on the mortgage and you're able to pay off the mortgage in full to the mortgage lender to whom you were paying the mortgage.

**Short Sale** – as the name implies, you sell your home and if your accepted purchase price is less than your mortgage balance (how much you owe on the original mortgage plus any arrears balance) you then need to negotiate (normally with the assistance of an attorney who specializes in this area) with your mortgage lender to accept the purchase price less any Realtor and attorney fees (if applicable). This is to your advantage because then *your lender* has *legally released you from any further debt and financial obligation* for *that property*. The lender will take all of the proceeds of a short sale; the sellers do not walk away with any money.

**Foreclosure** – when your home is foreclosed upon and the sheriff's sale takes place, many times the lender buys back the home from themselves then lists it for sale on the open market as "bank owned." Most or many times, the bank sells the home at a loss to them. That means that they sell the home for less than was owed to them. It is possible that the lender can sue the homeowners whom they foreclosed upon for the difference. As an example: Mr. and Mrs. Smith had their home sold at a sheriff's sale (foreclosure) and they owed $300,000. However, when the mortgage company they owed that mortgage balance to sold the house, they were only able to sell it for $250,000, but they had to pay Realtor fees and attorney fees totaling $20,000. Therefore, the mortgage lender will see that as a $70,000 loss to them and can potentially pursue Mr. and Mrs. Smith for that loss. Even if the mortgage lender says to the Smiths that they will forgive that loss, the Smiths should verify if that lender will do so in a manner which will cause them to have a tax implication. That means that the lender will send them a 1099 for the forgiven amount which can be added to the Smith's income and can cause them to owe the IRS on that amount as if it were earned income. Because of this aspect you need to contact your tax professional before accepting any offers of forgiveness of debt by any debtors.

For the aforementioned reason, as well as other potential liability risks, selling your home either traditionally or through a short sale agreement is the more finalized and cleaner alternative to foreclosure.

# Chapter 22

# Save On Your Energy Bills

## By Michael Menihan

Did you know that electric and natural gas service are no longer monopolies in many states, and due to government deregulation, you have a choice of who generates your electric and natural gas supplies? Maybe you do know because you have been getting annoying sales calls telling you to switch, but you might think it's a scam. Well, I am here to tell you that it's not, and you can save hundreds and maybe thousands of dollars a year depending on how much energy you consume in your home and/or small business.

**The Power to Choose**

Thanks to a national energy deregulation bill passed in 1999, in a number of states residential and small business customers can now manage and control their energy costs in ways never before thought possible. Before deregulation you had no choice. You did not need to pay attention to the energy markets and you simply paid your bill like everyone else. But today you have the power to choose your supplier! The savings will not come to you by default; you must actively make a choice. In a deregulated market you must decide whom to buy from, whether you should consider a market based (variable) rate or a (fixed) rate, where available. If you do not choose a new supplier, the local utility by default will remain the supplier of your energy at the highest market rate permitted.

**Electric - What was deregulated?**

Simply put, the supply portion of your electric bill, which is roughly 70% of the cost, was deregulated. The utilities sold off their power plants that generated the electricity, and now only own the transmission and distribution wires. They also serve as a 'default' for the supply to customers who do not shop for alternative electricity suppliers. With the move to competition, the utilities have separated their service into two parts:

- Regulated Distribution of Power (the Delivery), which is still only provided by the utility, and
- Supply, Bulk Generation Service (BGS), of the electric commodity, which is now open to competition.

Residential and Small Business customers (usually businesses consuming less than 10,000 kWh per month) who choose an alternate energy provider still have their power delivered, serviced, maintained and billed to them by their existing local utility. So the consumer doesn't experience any change in their electricity use; the only change will be the indication of the name of the alternative energy provider on the supply entry of their bill from the current utility provider.

**Natural Gas - What was deregulated?**

This works much like what was explained above. Likewise, this bill has two components, and the supply portion is the one where you can choose a new energy provider.

**Types of Programs**

If you have not chosen an alternate supplier you are paying a month-to-month variable rate based on filed tariffs for each service area. This is usually the most expensive rate that you can have since it is based upon the demand of the month in which you were billed. Like everything else in life, if you wait until the last minute to buy it you usually pay more. If you choose a new supplier you have the option of remaining on a month-to-month variable rate or choosing to lock in today's low rates for up to a year and sometimes longer. Energy costs are at or near their all-time lows so it makes sense to lock in for as long as you can to hedge rising energy costs and inflation.

## Types of Sales People

You might be contacted by a direct sales person for one supplier, a broker that represents multiple suppliers, a direct mail flyer urging you to call a number to switch energy suppliers, or you might hear a media (radio or TV) commercial. The sales person you deal with is paid a commission from the energy supplier as you pay your monthly bill, so there should be zero cost to you, the customer.

## How does it work?

Your salesperson might take your information over the phone, ask you to input your billing information on their website, or have you fill out an enrollment form. So when you are ready to choose a supplier, have your most recent energy bill in hand and ensure that you enter your information exactly as it appears on your current bill. If the information doesn't match your current bill exactly, your request could be rejected by your current utility/service provider. If you decide to start saving by choosing a new supplier, there should be no cost to switch. You get the same electricity or natural gas from the same delivery company (utility), using the same poles, same wires, same gas mains and the same meters. There will be no interruption or downtime of service. The only change will be a different supply provider's name appearing on your bill in 45-60 days. You will still pay the same utility company you always have; we call this a zero habit change service. Today's economy is difficult at best, so you owe it to yourself, at your residence and/or small business, to see if you can save money. You have nothing to lose and only savings to gain.

# Chapter 23

# Should I Pay Off My Mortgage Early?

## By Brian Cody, CFP

One of the trickiest questions to plague American homeowners who seek financial security is:

Should I pay off my home or keep my current mortgage?

There are three answers to this question:

- Yes, pay off the mortgage.
- No, keep the mortgage.
- Yes and no; do not pay it off immediately, but expedite the payment of your mortgage by creating a pay-off fund or paying a little extra during every payment cycle.

Some people like the peace of mind that comes with knowing that their mortgage company can no longer take away their home. For those people, paying off the house could make sense.

There are downsides to this solution:

- By paying off the mortgage, you could lose a potential tax write off.
- You have also tied up your money in real estate.
- What if you need the cash? You might find it more difficult to refinance a home when you are retired.

Other people simply want to maximize the cash flow created by their money.

With mortgage interest rates at historic lows, it is not too difficult to imagine getting better returns out of your money. For this reason, someone who is simply trying to maximize their income stream might decide to maximize their mortgage and use the leveraged money to increase cash flow.

There are downsides to this solution:

- Markets don't always move in the right direction.
- The stress of watching volatile markets can make it hard to enjoy your retirement.
- In some estate planning cases, it is better to pay off your home (e.g., Medicaid planning).

Finally, there are several different strategies that will help to expedite the payment of your mortgage. If you expedite the payment, you still have cash on the sidelines to invest.

- Some people add extra money to every mortgage payment, thereby reducing the length of the loan.

- Others create a mortgage pay-off fund. Raise money over time and you'll be able to use this money to pay off your mortgage at a pre-determined date.

It is always important to include an estate planning attorney and an accountant with these types of decisions.

Software can be utilized to show the financial difference between the various options; however, the financial software is only as good as the assumptions.

At the end of the day, the answer to this question usually comes down to the pre-retiree's gut. Yes, that's right; after weighing the facts, gut instincts can be an important aspect of financial planning. Naturally, seek the assistance of your trusted financial planner and tax advisor for advice on such an important matter.

# Chapter 24

# Reverse Mortgages: A Financial Option for Seniors

## By Zoltan Simon, Esq.

Debunking Myths Surrounding a Viable Financial Option for Homeowners 62 and Older

You have been taking care of your home for years; now your home can take care of you through a reverse mortgage. What is a reverse mortgage? A reverse mortgage is a federally insured home loan that allows homeowners 62 or older to convert a portion of their equity to cash. A reverse mortgage, in a nutshell, is a loan against your home where your payment is deferred while you or anyone on the mortgage lives in the home as their primary residence. This tool can help convert the equity in your home to cash without your having to make monthly mortgage payments, assisting you to better manage your financial future. With a reverse mortgage, rather than making monthly mortgage payments, you actually receive funds from the lender based on the terms you select. Perhaps best of all, a reverse mortgage allows you to still own your home throughout the entire term of your mortgage. This affords you the ability to retire on time.

This product was developed in Great Britain during the 1930s. The first known reverse mortgage in the United States was made in 1961 by Deering Savings & Loan. In 1981 the White House Conference on Aging recommended that "the FHA should develop an insurance program for reverse mortgage loans." In the United States, the first Home Equity Conversion Mortgage (HECM) was written in 1989 by James B. Nutter.

A reverse mortgage is an ideal situation for homeowners at least 62 years old that are house rich and cash poor. Also, a reverse mortgage will allow you to pass money onto a younger generation, such as your grandchildren when they currently need it the most, as opposed to later on. A reverse mortgage can also be used to purchase a new home through an HECM for Purchase. Created by the Housing & Economic Recovery Act of 2008, this is simply the process of applying the equity in your existing home toward the purchase of the new home with the benefit of only having one set of closing costs. If the old property does not have any FHA loan then you may even have the ability to retain both!

Social Security & Medicare are generally not affected by HECM proceeds. It would be prudent that everyone consult their federal benefits administrators or financial advisors.

This is a non-recourse loan; therefore, you will not be responsible for more than the lesser of the mortgage balance or 95% of market value. That means, if the property is sold to pay off the loan when the homeowner passes away or decides to leave the home for other reasons, the reverse mortgage debt will be paid off using the proceeds from the sale. In this scenario, the maximum amount owed will be the current market value of the house. What that means is if the home is upside down **NO** other asset in your estate will be in jeopardy. When you pass away, your heirs will have six months to sell the home and could be granted two three-month extensions.

Reverse mortgages have no time limit on how long seniors can stay in their homes. Since homeowners still own the property, lenders cannot evict them, provided they continue to live in and maintain their home, pay insurance and property taxes. The reverse mortgage can provide you with a source of funds to supplement your monthly income, cover rising healthcare costs, pay off existing mortgage to defer payment, any financial obligations, fix up your home, or simply gain peace of mind by not having a mortgage payment going forward.

Only primary residences are eligible for a reverse mortgage. A borrower must spend at least 183 days of the calendar year at the proposed collateral property. For a reverse purchase (HECM for Purchase), married spouses or other co-borrowers may be living apart because one of them is temporarily or permanently in a health care facility; however, at least one borrower must be living in the property in order for the loan to close.

**Benefits of a Reverse Mortgage:**
1. No monthly mortgage payment.
2. No income qualifications.
3. Loan Proceeds may be tax-free; consult tax advisor for more information.
4. Loan amount is not due until the last homeowner sells or permanently leaves the home.
5. Neither you nor your heirs will owe more money than your home's appraised market value at the maturity of the loan.
6. You decide how you would like to receive the loan proceeds:
   a. lump sum
   b. line of credit (can grow each year based on the equity and value of the market)
   c. monthly payment.

**Achieve your goal:**
With a reverse mortgage, you have the freedom and flexibility to use the money from your home in any manner you see fit. It's your money. Experience indicates that people use the funds for a variety of reasons including:

1. Healthcare and prescription drug costs.
2. Home remodel or repair.
3. Supplemental income for everyday living expenses.
4. Assisting grandchildren with education expenses.
5. Estate and financial planning.
6. Long-term care insurance.

Assistance is available to explain your various reverse mortgage options and help you determine if a reverse mortgage best addresses your financial needs. If you decide a reverse mortgage is the prudent solution, then the next step is determining which reverse mortgage program works best for your particular situation.

**Qualifying is easy:**
Although the process may vary by lender, there are typically no income or health qualifications and only minimal credit score requirements needed to qualify for a reverse mortgage.

The amount of reverse mortgage loan for which you qualify is determined by several factors, including but not limited to:

1. All homeowners must be at least 62.
2. Current appraised value.
3. Current interest rate.

The steps outlined below are intended to help you better understand each stage of the loan process.

1. **Get Educated**
   Borrowers are required to counsel with independent, third party counselors approved by the U.S. Department of Housing and Urban Development (HUD) in their local communities. Regardless of the reverse mortgage program you choose, counseling by a HUD approved counselor or an American Association of Retired Persons (AARP) approved counselor is required. The counselor is there to help you make sure that you are fully aware of your options and that you understand the reverse mortgage program and the loan process itself. Your lender can give

you a list of approved counseling agencies in your area. In addition to counseling, you should also seek advice from your family, legal and financial advisor.

2. **Appraisal**
   Upon completion and submission of your application, the lender will schedule an appraisal to determine the current market value of your home and whether or not any repairs are needed in order to meet loan underwriting guidelines.

3. **Underwriting**
   Underwriters will then review the loan file and appraisal in accordance with applicable FHA or lender loan policy. Upon completion, a representative of your lender will notify you of the lender's decision and inform you of any conditions that must be met prior to loan closing.

4. **Loan Closing**
   If approved, you will then decide how you want to receive your cash from the loan proceeds. The final step will be signing the documents at the loan closing. Disbursements of payment from your reverse mortgage loan may begin just days after closing by any of the following:
   a. lump sum
   b. line of credit
   c. monthly payment
   d. combination of any of these

5. **How much can be borrowed?**
   In most cases, maximum reverse mortgage loan amounts are based on the following factors:
   a. the age of the youngest homeowner
   b. the appraised value of your home
   c. the current interest rate
   d. the locally established lending limit

**Common Myths**

**Myth 1: Once I take out a reverse mortgage, the bank will own my home.**

**Fact: False.** Homeowners still retain title and ownership during the life of the loan. You can choose to sell the home at any time. As long as you continue to live in and maintain the home, pay the property taxes and homeowners insurance, the loan cannot be called due.

**Myth 2: There are restrictions on how reverse mortgage proceeds may be used.**

**Fact: False.** There are no restrictions. Do not work with any lender that is trying to use the proceeds to cross sell another product. I recommend that you do not work with any institution that even has the ability to cross sell anything.

**Myth 3: I won't qualify since I have an existing mortgage.**

**Fact: False.** The most common reason most homeowners 62 years and older take out a reverse mortgage is because they won't qualify for a cash out refinance or even a rate and term refinance. Therefore, the reverse mortgage is the best and only solution.

**Myth 4: If I outlive my life expectancy, the lender will evict me.**

**Fact: False.** As long as you continue to live in, maintain the home, and pay the taxes and insurance, you cannot be evicted.

**Myth 5: A reverse mortgage will affect my government benefits.**

**Fact:** A reverse mortgage generally does not affect regular Social Security or Medicare benefits. However, if you are on Medicaid, any reverse mortgage proceeds that you receive would count as an asset and could impact Medicaid eligibility. It is recommended that potential borrowers consult their federal benefits administrators or financial advisors to correctly structure the reverse as a lump sum or as a stream of payments.

**Myth 6: There are no objective advisors available to seniors trying to decide if a reverse mortgage suits their needs.**

**Fact: False.** You are required to work with independent, third-party HUD-approved counselors.

**Myth 7: My children will be responsible for the repayment of the loan.**

**Fact:** If the borrower or their estate wants to retain the property, the balance must be paid in full. There is no recourse if the borrower or their estate should sell the property for the fair market value if that value is less than the loan balance. If the property is sold for more than the loan balance, any remaining equity belongs to the borrower or their estate.

## Chapter 25

## Who knew cleaning toilets could boost self-esteem?

### By Fern Weis, Parent Coach & Educator

I once asked a mom about what her 13-year old son did to help around the house. "Oh, nothing," she replied. "All I ask is that he do his schoolwork and get good grades. I take care of the rest." That was already a tip-off to me about some of the difficulties in her family. In a way, this young man was allowed to call the shots and to believe that the world revolved around him. Let's get real. Grades are important, but they are not the only factor in determining self-confidence, self-esteem and future success.

High self-esteem does come from good grades, athletics, and performing arts, but there's more to this picture. Even the mundane – especially the mundane – can build a sense of self-worth and competence in children of all ages. Children must also know that their participation in all aspects of family life is important and appreciated. Let me start the list for you: mowing the grass, cleaning toilets, organizing a closet, clearing the table, doing laundry, putting away groceries, dusting, changing sheets. These are not just chores. They are life skills and confidence boosters. (Yes, I really did say that cleaning the toilet can boost your kid's confidence… as part of the bigger picture, of course.).

There's one thing you must do first: let go of your need for perfection and attention to detail. Although you can probably do it more efficiently yourself, it's time to sit on your hands and zip your lip. If the bed's not made perfectly, who cares? A few dust bunnies left after sweeping? Not important. Practice makes progress. You get help, and know that you're preparing your child for life after the cocoon of your home. He develops practical skills and feels competent. He may not enjoy the work, but it's necessary because:

1. He needs to know how to do these things.

2. You can use the help.

3. Every member of the family must contribute in some way.

4. He's part of something bigger than himself.

5. Not everything is fun. This is the real world.

6. He'll have a story to tell about something icky.

7. There's a sense of satisfaction when it's finally done.

8. One day he'll want this from his own kids!

I know you have a to-do list for the house. Who will be on your work crew today?

# Chapter 26

# Get Special Education Help for Students with Disabilities at No Cost

## By Darsi D. Beauchamp, Ph.D.

*"You must do the thing you think you cannot do."*
*Eleanor Roosevelt*

**SPECIAL EDUCATION**
Special Education is a necessary subject in the lives of our children in the United States (U.S.). The Supreme Court decision, Brown vs. Board of Education of Topeka, changed the face of politics and the educational arena. However, before 1965 there was a scarcity of any procedural safeguards for students with disabilities. In 1965, the Elementary and Secondary Education Act, PL 89-10, and the State Schools Act, PL 89-313, were enacted and provided funds to schools to help with the education of children with disabilities. In 1968, the Handicapped Children's Early Education Assistance Act, PL 90-538, was enacted to provide funds for children with disabilities in early childhood settings. In 1973, Section 504 of the

Rehabilitation Act was enacted and helped people with disabilities defend their civil rights with institutions that received federal monies, in addition to providing access to people with disabilities equitably. This Act, which is still in effect today, provides accommodations to students and people with disabilities. This Act also helped students with disabilities become integrated in schools and have access to activities and buildings. In 1975, the Education for All Handicapped Children Act (EHA), also known as PL 94-142, was enacted in response to the treatment of students with disabilities in institutions and schools. This Act made special education mandatory in the United States. In 1986, EHA was reauthorized as PL 99-457, to now be inclusive of children under age two (2) with disabilities and to create the Individual Family Service Plan (IFSP) for early intervention. In 1990, the Americans with Disabilities Act (ADA) provided protections from discrimination stemming from the Civil Rights Act of 1964 under five titles. Under the Clinton administration in 1997, EHA became the Individuals with Disabilities Education Act (IDEA), PL 105-17; it was revised under the Bush administration in 2004, and No Child Left Behind (NCLB) was also added. In 2008, the Children's Defense Fund indicated that 15% of our 3 year olds were enrolled in a state Pre-K, Head Start or special education program and that 38.8% of our 4 year olds were also enrolled in those programs.

## IDEA

The EHA had been enacted to provide students with disabilities access to the public schools. IDEA, on the other hand, provided that researched-based interventions and methods be used, as well as full participation in the public school system, which also included independent living skills, eventually leading to a self-sufficient economic life for children with disabilities. IDEA assured students received services from ages 3 to 21 in the school system. IDEA also added new categories to the disabilities range, such as autism, traumatic brain injury, and Attention Deficit Hyperactivity Disorder (ADHD). IDEA presented that a functional behavioral assessment (FBA) and a behavioral intervention plan (BIP) be provided to students whose behavior stood in the way of their learning and the learning of their peers. Furthermore, IDEA also added transition plans to help students with disabilities transition from secondary schools to adult life, or even into higher education or post-secondary education.

## NO CHILD LEFT BEHIND (NCLB)

No Child Left Behind (NCLB) is a revision of the Elementary and Secondary Education Act of 2001, PL 107-110. This Act requires that schools, teachers, and administrators be accountable for how the students perform in the schools, including children of special and bilingual education. It requires highly qualified teachers teaching the students and adequate yearly progress of students. The Act, although under revision in the current administration, required that school districts reach a 100% proficiency in the areas of math and reading by the year 2012. Thus, each state has developed goals and objectives or benchmarks for each grade level and each subject matter, and tests in these areas, which are now published for parents to peruse. This Act also added the Assistive Technology Act (ATA) of 2004, PL 108-364. The ATA provides funds to schools to purchase assistive technology that will help students with disabilities in their educational endeavors, as well as in their transition phase within their individualized education plan (IEP). The funds are divided into different Titles: Title I- Improving the Academic Achievement of the Disadvantaged, Title II - Preparing, Training, and Recruiting High Quality Teachers and Principals, Title III - Language Instruction for Limited English Proficient and Immigrant Students, Title IV - 21st Century Schools, Title V - Promoting Informed Parental Choice.

## FAPE and LRE

Under IDEA, children have many laws that protect them. Some of the laws and regulations, in other words rights, include LRE and FAPE. LRE is the Least Restrictive Environment and FAPE is Free Appropriate Public Education. FAPE is deemed as the proper educational program that is intended for the child's individual needs, and in which the child is prepared in school educationally for employment and independent living skills. FAPE is an appropriate program, not the best program. In other words, the U.S. Supreme Court deemed that children of special education were entitled to an appropriate program, not the best possible program. As parents we feel that we want the best for our children, but sometimes the best in education may be viewed as over the top and school districts must assure that the child's educational program provides a learning environment in which the children will make meaningful progress educationally. This also means that the child, no matter the disability, has the ability to learn and requires the opportunity to do so. Under FAPE, there are other procedural safeguards such as related services that a child may need to help with their disability as well as in support of their disability. Some of these programs are: Speech/Language Therapy, Physical Therapy (PT), Occupational Therapy (OT), Psychological services, parent training, health services, transportation, transitional services.

## BILINGUAL EDUCATION

Title VI of the Civil Rights Act of 1964 provided rights to students in need of bilingual education (also called English Language Learners [ELL], Limited English Proficient [LEP], and English as a Second Language [ESL] students). This Act provides rights to access based on color and race. Nonetheless, it was not until the Supreme Court decision of Lau v. Nichols that made headway in helping Chinese students in the San Francisco, California area overcome their language barriers and access to education. In New Jersey, when there are 20 students of a particular language with needs, bilingual education must be provided. Parents have a right to sign to have their children serviced and also have a right to sign their children *out of the program*. Nonetheless, the two-prong situation arises when the student is in need of bilingual education and of special education services, and the schools may not have the appropriate personnel to service the children. It is important to note that the law requires equal access and protection; therefore, the students must receive testing in their native language (students may have difficulty with these tests, since they have not been instructed in that language, and are deficient and even illiterate in that language; therefore, results may not be optimal), instruction in their native language when the materials should also be offered to parents in their native language, and there should be an interpreter in the IEP meeting.

# EARLY INTERVENTION PROGRAM (EIP)

Early Intervention is a service for children with disabilities or delays from birth, who are eligible from 0 to 3 years of age. A family coordinator is sent to the home to plan with the family and come up with an Individual Family Service Plan (IFSP). A social worker is also sent to the home to offer service referrals to the parents. Language Interpreters are available with the state upon request. The services may include physical therapy, occupational therapy, speech and language, nursing, special education services, and Applied Behavioral Analysis (ABA) therapy services, to name a few. The IFSP provides information on who will be providing the services, when and how often the services will be provided, and the goals and objectives for the child regarding the services. The service providers are experts in the areas of services and come to the home and provide services according to the IFSP. Every month, the service coordinators have a family training meeting to provide the family with an update on the goals and objectives from the plan (explaining growth) and which new goals and objectives will be worked on for the following month. The family service coordinator meets with the family every six (6) months to review and renew the IFSP to determine new goals and objectives and whether the number of hours should be increased or decreased for the therapies. When your child is close to three (3) years of age, the family coordinator will have a transition meeting with the school's Child Study Team (CST) (please be aware that you need to register your child in the school district where you are domiciled before the coordination with the Child Study Team begins). The family coordinator also sends the child's records with a summary report to the CST for their review. The family coordinator may also participate in the initial IEP meeting to help develop the initial IEP for your child. The services under this program are free, but some fees may apply according to family resources. If the family is of low resources, they can also apply for Supplemental Security Income (SSI) from the Social Security Administration (SSA) for the child; this is also paired with Medicaid to pay for additional services and medical care. Lastly, when the child turns three (3) years of age, the family coordinator sends the early intervention case to the state's Home Care Program, which commences during the transition from early intervention to the school district. The Home Care Program assigns a case manager who will coordinate continuing therapy services (various hospitals offer the therapy services) via telephone calls, and not necessarily through visits to the home.

## PRESCHOOL

As we mentioned before, all children with and without disabilities are to receive a Free and Appropriate Public Education (FAPE). Children who have disabilities can begin school at age three (3). Pre-School children with disabilities must be treated the same as any school-aged child. They are eligible to be in the Least Restrictive Environment (LRE); therefore, they have a right to be educated with their peers, unless the IEP Team (inclusive of the parents) decides that the child will benefit from a Pre-School Handicapped program. Nonetheless, the code is clear that children with disabilities should be placed with their peers and be in an all-inclusive program to the maximum extent possible. In addition, the children should be evaluated and the IFSP should become a record, along with any evaluation from a health care provider or specialist which indicates that the child has a disability, and recommendations by those specialists. The school district can conduct their own evaluations, but cannot decline other evaluations. Furthermore, once the parents sign to consent for evaluations, the school has 90 days to conclude the evaluations and to provide the student with an initial IEP. The programming must be ready to be implemented by age three (3). This means that in order for the school district to conform to having the child begin school by age three (3), they must begin the referral and evaluations 120 days before the child becomes three (3) years of age. Nonetheless, the initial IEP cannot be implemented if the parents do not sign it. However, the parents can sign as participants and for the eligibility as well as to commence services, but still can invoke the 15 days to review the IEP. If within the 15 days, the parents do not agree with the district they may subscribe to the procedural safeguards such as mediation and due process. Once the child turns three (3), the school district cannot deny him/her entrance to school, especially knowing that the child has a disability.

## *HOW TO QUALIFY FOR SPECIAL EDUCATION* REFERRAL

Once you, a doctor, a teacher, an administrator, or anyone refers (in writing to the school principal and/or director of special education) a student to the Child Study Team (CST) for evaluations, the CST has 20 days to coordinate a meeting with the parents and the entire IEP Team to discuss the referral and to make a determination to evaluate. Remember, you can suspect, not always know, there is a problem with a student not making proper progress in school.

## IEP TEAM

The IEP Team consists of the parents, a school psychologist, a learning disabilities teacher consultant (LDTC), a social worker, a special education teacher, a general education teacher, a speech therapist (if warranted), a physical therapist (if warranted), and an occupational therapist (if warranted). One of the providers, whether the school psychologist, the LDTC, or the social worker, will also become the case manager for the IEP team. There could be a representative from the school district, which can very well be a principal, vice-principal, director of special services, or the board attorney (if warranted); these members must also be knowledgeable on supervision and the curriculum. However, any member must be familiar with the child and the child's educational strengths, weaknesses, and performance. If a child is 14 years and over (the child with disabilities can be in school until age 21), they too can be a member of the IEP Team. In addition, in order to coordinate services with pertinent agencies, a representative of those agencies can also be present, especially if they are coordinating transition services for the student. Furthermore, a parent has a right to bring an expert, friend, relative, advocate, or attorney to the IEP meeting.

## MEETINGS

All meetings should be preceded by a notification by mail and another adequate form to the parent, with copies of a proposed IEP and/or evaluations to the parent 10 days before the IEP meeting. The notification should indicate the date, time, location, reason, and who will be attending the IEP meeting. All IEP meetings can be recorded by the parent. There is no need to ask permission; however, out of courtesy to the school district and so they too can have the same opportunity to record, they should be informed in advance.

## EVALUATIONS

Initial evaluations are done when the child is in school (except for the initial evaluation – see the Pre-School section) within the 90 calendar days' timeframe after the parents have signed a consent to evaluate. While the evaluations are going on within those 90 days, the school can provide interventions as developed by the Intervention and Referral Services Team (I&RS). However, the I&RS Team cannot stand in the way of the referral to the Child Study Team. The Child Study Team should also include the school nurse in the initial evaluation to provide the student with a physical assessment and medical referrals, if necessary, to rule out any medical conditions that may be standing in the way of the child's learning, including evaluations done by a neurologist or a neurodevelopmental pediatrician. If the child's behavior stands in the way of his/her learning and the learning of others, then a Functional Behavioral Assessment (FBA) and Behavioral Intervention Plan (BIP) shall be conducted again with the consent of the parents, because it is an evaluation. Teachers can use different forms of evaluations in the classroom to document if the interventions they have attempted to use with a child have been working or if, despite the interventions, the students still have problems in progressing. The tests for assessment in the classroom are Dynamic Indicators of Basic Literacy Skills (DIBELS), Developmental Reading Assessment (DRA), Wechsler Individual Achievement Test (WIAT), Curriculum-Based Measurements (CBM), and Response to Intervention (RTI) – CBM is a part of this as well. All evaluations that are conducted at the school district are done at the expense of the public school system.

## RE-EVALUATIONS

All re-evaluations are done within a three (3) year time frame to demonstrate the growth of the child and to reformulate the IEP. Re-evaluations can occur sooner if warranted. The school district has 45 days to conduct the re-evaluations. The results should be provided to parents in an IEP meeting where new goals and objectives, as well as short-term benchmarks, are developed.

## INDEPENDENT EDUCATIONAL EVALUATIONS (IEE)

During the discussion of the evaluations or re-evaluations, if the parents are not in agreement with the results, they can then invoke in writing their right to IEEs. The school district has 20 days to respond to the parents whether they will accept the IEEs, or whether they will then file a due process hearing defending their evaluations. If the school district does not file for a due process hearing, they then must provide the parents with a list of providers that are just as qualified as the school evaluators, in other words with the same qualifications and certifications. The parents can choose from the list or can choose an independent evaluator from outside the list. The IEEs are at public expense and the parents do not pay for them. Even if the school district files for a due process, the parents can still have the independent educational evaluations done, but must pay for them out of pocket. Nonetheless, the IEEs recommendations and summaries must be taken into consideration by the school district. No school district can interfere with an IEE as per federal code. The school district or the school board attorney cannot ask the independent evaluators to refrain from providing recommendations or which test to administer. This would be construed as an interference. It is not advisable for parents to have the independent evaluations done in the school setting in order to avoid interference, and in order to give the student the opportunity to perform outside of the school district, unless the evaluator must observe the student in the school to gather data for their report, or is evaluating the child's programming and placement. The IEEs should be done at the office of the evaluator, in the home of the child, or at an approved site per code. If for any reason the evaluation being requested by the parent has not been done by the school district, then the school district has 45 days to evaluate the child; if the parents are still in disagreement, they can still have the IEE done at public expense. Remember that no independent evaluator can be employed by the district in which the child is domiciled, but an evaluator from another district can evaluate the child. You are only entitled to one independent evaluation in each area that you are in disagreement with every time the school district performs an evaluation or reevaluation that you disagree with. A student should be evaluated every three (3) years, but does not have to be if both the parents and school district agree to waive the evaluations.

## CLASSIFICATION

Once the IEP Team determines that a child is eligible for special education services, they must determine which of the 13 categories the child falls under to receive proper educational interventions. For complete determinations, see N.J.A.C. 6A:14-3.5; this is an excerpt of the listing under this code.

## CLASSIFICATION, ACRONYM, DETERMINATION

<u>Specific Learning Disability</u> (SLD) Perceptually impaired in language, imperfect ability to listen, think, speak, read, write, spell, math calculations. <u>Speech and Language Impairment</u> (SI) Speech disorder in articulation, phonology, fluency, voice, or any combination. <u>Other Health Impaired</u> (OHI) Chronically ill – disability characterized by limited strength, vitality, or alertness in educational environment due to chronic or acute health problems. <u>Emotional Disturbance</u> (ED) Multiple characteristics in intellectual, sensory, health, interpersonal relationships, and behaviors or feelings that are inappropriate; pervasive mood of unhappiness or depression, tendency to develop physical symptoms or fears. <u>Auditorily (Hearing) Impaired</u> (AI/HI) Inability to hear within normal limits. <u>Autistic</u> Pervasive developmental disability impacting verbal and non-verbal communication and social interaction, which adversely affects a student's performance. <u>Cognitive Impaired</u> (CI) "Mentally retarded" (three levels included; see below) Average general cognitive functioning 1. Mild CI: Educable-level of cognitive development and adaptive behavior; mildly below age expectations. 2. Moderate CI: Trainable-level of cognitive development and adaptive behavior; moderately below age expectations. 3. Severe Cognitive CI: Severe Impairment; eligible for day training. Cognitive development and adaptive behavior

severely below age expectations. Communication Impairment handicapped-language disorder in areas of morphology, syntax, semantics, and/or pragmatics/discourse, not due to auditory impairment. Multiply Disabled (MD) Multiply handicapped, multiple disabilities, two or more disabling conditions. Deaf-blindness (DB) Concomitant hearing and visual impairments; severe communication needs. Orthopedically Impaired (OI) Severe orthopedic impairments. Pre-School child with a disability Between ages of 3 and 5, handicapped with a developmental delay. Social Maladjustment (SM) Inability to conform to standards of behavior established by school. Traumatic Brain Injury (TBI) Neurologically impaired; injury caused to the brain by external force or insult to the brain. Visually Impaired (VI), Visually Handicapped – impairment, even with correction.

## INDIVIDUALIZED EDUCATIONAL PLAN ("IEP")

The IEP must be developed within 30 calendar days from the determination that a child is eligible for special education and the related services determined by the evaluations. Parts of an IEP are as follows:

1. Strengths and areas to be addressed academically, developmentally, and functionally
2. Any concerns the parents may have about their child's education
3. Any results from assessments and evaluations
4. Behavioral interventions for students whose behavior stands in the way of their learning and the learning of others
5. ESL or LEP classes for children with limited English proficiency.
6. Blind or visual impairment – Braille instruction in coordination with the Commission for the Blind
7. Communication needs
8. Academic levels
9. Assistive Technology devices needs and services
10. Involvement of DDD
11. Involvement of DVRS from age 14 or younger or other agencies

12. Statement of present levels of academic achievement
13. LRE-involvement in general education and how disability affects involvement and progress
14. Measurable annual academic and functional goals and short term goals if APA
15. Supplementary aids and services
16. Related services
17. Individual modifications
18. Frequency, location, duration of related services and modifications
19. From age 14 to 21, graduation requirements and how student is expected to meet them
20. Types of assessments and any modifications
21. Transitions: elementary to middle, middle to high school, high school to work world, including social, academic, and vocational statements
22. At age 16 or younger, measurable post-secondary goals, which include training, education, and employment
23. Independent living or community participation also included
24. Progress of goals and objectives
25. How parents will be informed of progress
26. Information on out of district placements and how student will participate with nondisabled peers
27. How district will include participation of agencies at IEP meetings
28. Meetings annually to review IEP
29. Review of annual goals
30. Review of re-evaluations, if any
31. Classroom/teacher assessments review, state assessments, observations, etc.
32. Any new needs as presented by IEP Team, inclusive of parents and teacher
33. Review of out of district placements if can come back, transition to least restrictive environment
34. Signatures of those who participated in IEP meeting
35. Remember that the IEP must first be completed before placement is decided

36. The school district may bring forth to the meeting an outline of what will be offered; however, the IEP must be developed during the IEP Team meeting.
37. The proposed IEP and any evaluations must be sent to the parents 10 days before the meeting along with a notice of meeting.

## EXTENDED SCHOOL YEAR (ESY)

This part of the instructional aspect of a child's IEP demonstrates that during the summer months, the child may regress and how long the student would take to recover, that a part of the child's learning needs to be continued, or that their behavioral or physical conditions warrant the related services. The usual time frame is for the entire month of July. Some programs can go up to the second week of August in private schools.

## PLACEMENT

The goals, objectives, the statements, the entire IEP must be developed before placement can be determined. Remember that the IEP is a legal working document that can be amended at any time, even if new benchmarks can be added when the placement is determined.

## SECTION 504 ACCOMMODATION PLAN

Students who do not qualify under IDEA and have disabilities qualify for the American with Disabilities Act (ADA) Section 504 Rehabilitation Act; however, all children who qualify for IDEA also qualify under Section 504. The Section 504 also covers adults in the work environment. A disabled person under ADA "has a physical or mental impairment which substantially limits one or more major life activities; has a record of such impairment; or is regarded as having such an impairment." The children have a disability, but not a learning disability or impairment. Usually an ADA Section 504 Accommodation Plan is used for students who have physical impairments (permanent or temporary) or asthma, epilepsy, allergies, ADHD, diabetes, central auditory processing problems, physical therapy and occupational therapy needs, any related services or accommodations, modifications, or special education services that are not eligible under an IDEA with an IEP. The students are still required to have FAPE and LRE just as in IDEA. A Section 504 committee meets to evaluate the needs of a child and to receive the medical documentation from parents to prepare a plan. The recommendations of the health care provider are taken into consideration and provided in the plan.

## GUARDIANSHIP

This means providing for the protection of a person who is incapacitated or incapable of making financial, educational, and medical decisions on their own. Custody usually ends for the child's parents when the child is 18 years old. The incapacitated child does not have the capability of managing their own affairs. Children's guardianship can also be obtained by a person other than a parent in special circumstances with minor typical and atypical children. The parents do not lose their parental rights; however, the guardian is the person making the decisions in the upbringing of the child, up until the court deems the guardianship is no longer needed and is no longer in the best interest of the child or children. However, the court appoints an attorney who will interview the parties mentioned in the verified complaint. The courts in New Jersey also require a 90-day accounting report and an annual report to be submitted by the guardians.

## *PROCEDURAL SAFEGUARDS* MANIFESTATION DETERMINATION

A special education student is not excused from school rules or board regulations for behavioral issues. However, a special education student is entitled to a manifestation determination meeting to determine whether or not the act committed stemmed from their disability. If the act committed stemmed from their disability, then the student is entitled to a manifestation determination and then a board hearing with the board of education to present their evidence on their behalf. If the act committed does not stem from the disability, then the student may receive the same suspension as a student in regular education. Nonetheless, if a parent does not agree with the manifestation determination, they can attend the board hearing and go further with an expedited due process hearing within 20 days after the hearing is filed. The administrative law judge (ALJ) makes the determination within fifteen (15) days from the time the due process is received. Any time a special education child is suspended for ten (10) school days, there may be a change of placement. This means that a school can place the child in an alternative setting for 45 days. If the school filing to end the placement is the out of district school, that school cannot unilaterally end the placement.

## MEDIATION

This avenue is used to have a state employee who is trained in mediation attend a mediation meeting with the two parties in dispute. The state employee is employed by the Department of Education, Office of Special Education Programs (OSEP), and is an impartial party to help assist the parties with the dispute in reaching an agreement. The OSEP mediators are knowledgeable of the federal and state codes under IDEA, N.J.A.C.6A-14 et seq., and ADA. The mediation, unlike the court mediations, is at no cost to the parents. The parents may bring with them experts, an attorney, or an advocate. The Stay Put provision is also valid during the mediation procedure. If mediation does not become the viable solution and a school district maintains that they want to remove the student from their placement or not enforce the IEP, then the parents can file for emergent relief.

## EMERGENT RELIEF

This provision is a serious procedural safeguard, and one must provide evidence that the removal or non-compliance can cause the child "irreparable" harm before a full hearing is heard. The Stay Put provision comes into play at this point until the matter is heard either in the emergent relief hearing, or transferred to the due process avenue and this has concluded. The parents must provide evidence that the irreparable harm will occur if the relief is not granted, legal right of claim is settled, that the claim can stand on its own merits, or that the child will suffer harm more than the school district if they cannot acquire the relief.

## DUE PROCESS

If you file for emergent relief for one issue and your petition has several other issues that are not a part of the emergent relief, they then become a part of the due process. During the due process, a resolution meeting is scheduled within 15 days of receipt of the packet by all parties. During the resolution meeting, all parties must be in agreement to record the meeting. If the parents have an attorney, then the board attorney may be present. If the parents are represented by a non-attorney advocate, then the board attorney cannot be present. The case manager, the director of special services, the supervisor of special education, even the superintendent may be present. However, this is not an IEP team meeting, so the child study team should not interfere with the process. This is not about offering services, developing an IEP, or arguing about the petition. This meeting is to discuss the issues presented to the state by the parents on how the disputed issues can be solved as written in the petition. Once the issues are agreed upon, a settlement agreement is drafted by hand the day of the meeting. The formal settlement agreement can be drafted by either party. If on the day of the resolution meeting the issues are still outstanding, or only part of the issues are still outstanding, the case can be scheduled for a conference with the judge at the office of administrative law in Newark or Trenton, depending on the location of the school district. The judge will give another opportunity to have the pending issues discussed and come to a resolution that day in court. If the issues are not resolved that day, then the judge will schedule the case for a hearing. Usually the parties can have access to the assigned administrative law judge on the telephone for phone conferences to help resolve the issues. Experts, witnesses, and discovery of documents are a part of the due process procedures, as well as subpoenas of teachers and other school staff. If the case is settled upon an agreement, the board of education must vote on a resolution that will be sent to the court so that the court can approve the settlement agreement with an order from the judge. If the settlement agreement is not adhered to, the parents can return to court to have it enforced. Reimbursement of attorney fees can be formally sought if the parent has prevailed during the due process hearing.

## COMPLAINTS

Parents are entitled to file a complaint investigation with the Department of Education. The complaint is based on violations of the federal or state code within one year of its occurrence. The Department of Education will investigate within 60 days. The facts are presented to the state and the determination is made within the 60 days. If for any reason the parents also file a due process petition, the due process procedure must first occur before the state begins the complaint. At this point, the state will provide an "exceptional circumstances" extension of time until the due process procedures have concluded. If the issues are resolved and rectified during the due process procedures, then the decision of the court or the settlement agreement is binding. If there is only a complaint investigation, then the state may visit the district and interview parties and compile records to make the determination on how the district can compensate the child with corrective procedures. The Department of Education will also provide the school district technical assistance on how to correct the outstanding issues. If the parents want to appeal the complaint investigation results, they must do so via a due process, for there is no appeal process of complaint investigations. A two year period is the allotted time to file due process commencing with the date of the filed complaint.

## *COORDINATING WITH AGENCIES IN NJ*

It is important for parents to note that all children with disabilities must be registered by them with the Division of Developmental Disabilities (DDD) for them to appraise the child for services. The Division of Vocational Rehabilitation Services (DVRS) is a consultative body for students 14 years of age and older to help in the transition phase of students with disabilities from school to work programs. The DVRS will conduct vocational assessments for high school students with disabilities to better understand and propose a work plan according to the child's strengths, needs, and aspirations. Both the DDD and DVRS should be invited by the school to IEP meetings. In addition, the DVRS, in coordination with other agencies depending on the disability of the student, will devise a transition plan that will help teach the student in the areas of assistive technology, vocational assessments, community based instruction (provided by the school district), transition instruction (provided by the school district), independent living skills, and social skills.

## *LIST OF AGENCIES AS PROVIDED BY THE NJ EARLY INTERVENTION SYSTEM (Reproduced with permission of NJEIS, 2010).* Statewide Agencies:

*Advocacy:*

Disability Rights New Jersey, (800) 922-7233; www.drnj.org

Statewide Parent Advocacy Network (SPAN, (800)654-SPAN; www.spannj.org

Education Law Center; www.edlawcenter.org

NJ Coalition for Inclusive Education, (732) 613-0400; www.njcie.net

Wrights Law, www.wrightslaw.com

*Assistive Technology*

NJ Protection & Advocacy, (800) Dial-Tec; www.njpanda.org

NJ Coalition for the Advancement of Assistive & Rehab Technology; http://www.njcart.org/

Rehabilitation Technology Services and Technology Lending Center (CPNJ); (888) 322-1918

Disability Resources for Assistive Technology; http://www.disabilityresources.org/AT.html

Assistive Technology Center (Advancing Opportunities); http://www.assistivetechnologycenter.org/tlc/tlc.php

Family Resource Connection, Inc.; http://frainc.org/techconnection/

*Child Care:*

NJ Inclusive Childcare Project, (800) 654-7726 x108; www.spannj.org/njiccp

County Childcare Resource and Referral Agencies, (800) 3-329-2273; www.njaccrra.org

*Disabilities:*

The Arc of New Jersey, (732) 246-2525; www.arcnj.org

Council on Developmental Disabilities, (800) 216-1199; www.njddc.org

Division on Developmental Disabilities, (800) 832-9173; www.state.nj.us/humanservices

National Information Center for Children & Youth with Disabilities, (800)695-0285; www.nichcy.org

*Early Intervention:*

New Jersey Early Intervention System, (888) 653-4463; www.njeis.org

*Education:*

NJ Dept. of Education, (609)292-4469; www.state.nj.us/education
NJ Dept of Early Childhood Education, 609-777-2074; www.nj.gov/education/ece

Head Start Programs;
www.state.nj.us/humanservices/oece/head_start.htm
NJ Dept. of Special Education, (609)292-4469;
www.nj.gov/education/specialed

The Learning Resource Centers, (609)292-4469; www.nj.gov/education/lrc

Individuals with Disabilities Education Act (IDEA); www.ideapractices.org

*Family Support:*

Family Support Center of NJ, (800) FSC-NJ10; www.fscnj.org

NJ Self-Help Clearinghouse, (800) 367-6274; http://www.njgroups.org

Exceptional Parent Resource Guide, (800)EPARENT; www.eparent.com

Options Manual (800) FSC-NJ10; www.fscnj.org

*Health Care:*

Community Health Law Project (888)838-3180; http://www.chlp.org

Family Voices (Health Issues): (800 )654-SPAN x110; www.familyvoices@spannj.org

NJ Family Care (Health Coverage) (800)701-0710; www.njfamilycare.org

*Parent to Parent Support:*

National Father's Network; www.fathersnetwork.org

NJ Statewide Parent to Parent: (908)537-467; email: parent2parent@spannj.org

*Social Services:*

Women, Infants and Children (WIC) (800) 328-3838; www.state.nj.us/health/fhs/wic/index.shtml

Division of Youth and Family Services (DYFS) 877-652-2873; www.state.nj.us/humanservices/dyfs Special

Child Health Services (888) 653-4463
Supplemental Security Disability Insurance (800) 772-1213; www.ssa.gov

*Transition Resources:*

Boggs Center, (732) 235-9300; http://rwjms.umdnj.edu/boggscenter

National Early Childhood Technical Assistance Center (NECTAC); www.nectac.org

The following is an informal listing of resources that have information about services and supports that many families may find useful. The NJEIS does not endorse any content, program, product or methodology found on any of their listed websites. All resources were accurate at the time of printing.

## DISABILITY RELATED/SPECIFIC RESOURCES:

*Autism:*

Autism NJ, (800) 4-Autism; www.autismnj.org (formerly COSAC)

Autism Speaks, (888) 777-6227; www.autismspeaks.org

Autism Society of America, (800)328-8476; www.autism-society.org

*Visual Impairment:*

Commission for the Blind and Visually Impaired (973)648-3333 (Central Office); www.state.nj.us/humanservices/cbvi/home

National Federation of the Blind, (410)659-9314; www.nfb.org

American Foundation for the Blind, (800)232-5463; www.afb.org

*Cerebral Palsy:*
Cerebral Palsy of NJ (Advancing Opportunities), (888) 322-1918; www.cpofnj.org

United Cerebral Palsy of Northern, Central and Southern NJ, 908-879-2243; www.ucp.org/ucp_local.cfm/100

*Hearing Impairment:*
Division of Deaf and Hard of Hearing, (800)792-8339; www.state.nj.us/humanservices/ddhh

*Down Syndrome:*
National Down Syndrome Society (NDSS), (800)221-4602; www.ndss.org

National Down Syndrome Congress (NDSC), (800)232-NDSC; www.ndsccenter.org

The Arc of NJ, (732)246-2525; www.arcnj.org

The Judy Center for Down Syndrome (healthcare); (201)996-JUDY Down Syndrome Association of Central NJ, (866) 369-6796; www.dsacnj.org

Down Syndrome Web Page; www.downsyndrome.com

*Fragile X Syndrome:*
The National Fragile X Foundation, (800)688-8765; www.FragileX.org

The Fragile X Association of NJ, www.fragilex.org/htm/new_jersey.htm

*Rare Disorders:*
Rare Disorders, http://www.rare-disorders.com/

Disability Resources; http://www.disabilityresources.org/RARE.html

*Spina Bifida:*
Spina Bifida Assoc. of the Tri- State region, (908)782-7475;
www.sbatsr.org

*Sibling Resources:*
The Sibling Support Project, (206)297-6368;
www.siblingsupport.org

Parents and Agencies Supporting Siblings (PASS); (908)537-4673

Frequently Asked Questions Siblings Need to Know About their Brother or Sister with Special Needs: For a copy, contact Mid-Jersey Cares REIC (732)937-5437

Transition Resources:

"Special Needs Successful Inclusion: A Guide to Planning Community Activities for Children with Special Needs": To order, go to www.cnjmchc.org

NECTAC: Transition
www.nectac.org/topics/transition/transition.asp
NECTAC: Inclusion www.nectac.org/inclusion

*"... Laws and institutions must go hand in hand with the progress of the human mind. As that becomes more developed, more enlightened, as new discoveries are made, new truths disclosed, and manners and opinions change with the change of circumstances, institutions must advance also, and keep pace with the times. We might as well require a man to wear still the coat which fitted him when a boy, as civilized society to remain ever under the regimen of their barbarous ancestors."*
–Thomas Jefferson

## Chapter 27

# Are you crippling your kids? Tough love Rx for parents

### By Fern Weis, Parent Coach & Educator

When you rescue, fix or overindulge kids, they begin to believe that they cannot do for themselves. They question their own worth and competence. They depend more on you, less on themselves. This is when you begin to label them as lazy, unmotivated and apathetic, with no sense of self or purpose. Is this what you really want for them, and for you? to be takers and enablers?

Sometimes I have to do the "tough love" thing with parents. You may be annoyed with me for pushing you, but you can take it, and so can I. It's not just teenagers I'm talking about. These patterns start much earlier and parents are the culprits. (I'm saying "you," and please understand that I've been there, too.)

\* When your child makes a mistake and you criticize or judge, you belittle. When you find the **learning opportunity**, you **empower.**

\* When you give her more than she needs, she will take things for granted. When you give her what she needs and **have her work towards what she wants,** she will **learn commitment, responsibility, appreciation and gratitude.**

\* When you ask your child for help and your perfectionist nature says, 'not good enough,' you diminish. When you are hurried and frazzled and end up doing it yourself, you diminish. When you **accept help** and **praise the effort,** you empower.

\* When you are the benevolent or terrified fixer, you send the message that he is helpless and should be scared of life. When you encourage him to t**ake a chance, maybe even fail,** he hears that he is **capable and resilient.**

\* When you give in or give up because it's easier than dealing with wheedling and whining, you encourage self-centered, manipulative, even helpless behavior. When you **stand your ground and set limits**, kids learn to **manage frustration and deal with disappointment.**

You are not powerless to influence your children, even though some days you feel that way. Every day, in every moment, you have the power and opportunity to move them a step closer to confidence and independence, and higher self-esteem. Will you take it?

Reflection/Action

1. Where do you see unproductive attitudes in your children? In you?

2. What would you like to see instead?

3. When do you ignore your "inner guidance system"? Are you angry, hungry, worried, fearful, in a rush?

4. Think of a time when you enabled or overindulged your child. What did he learn? How might you handle that situation differently the next time?

## Chapter 28

# It's not your job to make sure your kids are happy

### By Fern Weis, Parent Coach & Educator

I love Pharrell Williams' song "Happy." It's an upbeat, catchy tune, and you have to love the videos of all those people dancing.

But... in real life, there's way too much emphasis on our kids striving to be happy. It just breaks your heart when they're sad or disappointed, doesn't it? And yet, it's inevitable. As much as you'd like to, you can't prevent it. We all know there is unpleasantness in life. In fact, you'd probably admit that those difficult times made you stronger. But back to your kids. If you can't control it, what is your role? You have the power to guide them through it when the inevitable happens. This is the greatest gift of all. Let's take a closer look.

There's a crazy belief, and it spread like wildfire, that kids must be happy all the time, that it's not okay to be feeling whatever is, well, the opposite. Trophies for the winning and losing teams, intervening with teachers, offering food and 'things' to compensate for loss, saying 'yes' when you ought to say 'no', encouraging them to be upbeat when they're sad… they don't bring true happiness (whatever that word means).

I, too, have been guilty of saying to my kids, "I just want you to be happy." Of course I want them to be happy. But if there's one thing I know I can't guarantee for them, it's that.

Then what is your job in the drama of their lives?

Your job is… to hold their hand when they're miserable.

Your job is… to walk with them through sadness and disappointment.

Your job is… to express confidence that they can get through it.

Your job is… to help them figure out how to bounce back.

Your job is… to guide them in finding healthy ways to cope.

Your job is… to be their parent.

## Chapter 29

# College Prep Goes On for Years: Taking the Angst Out of the Apps

### By Fern Weis, Parent Coach & Educator

Back in the dark ages of the 1970s, preparing for college was a lot simpler. I paid attention to which courses I would take, but for a soon-to-be liberal arts major, I didn't have too much planning to do. Most of us took our SATs once, perhaps an advanced placement test, and applied to five or six schools. Then we went on with our lives while waiting for the letters to come, in the mail. Yes, in an envelope, straight to the mailbox.

Today, course selection begins in middle school, so your student can get into the right courses in high school. Some middle schools host college representatives. Seniors check online, endlessly, to find out the very moment the results are in. Students apply to a dozen colleges, changing the odds of who is accepted. There are services and consultants to help them prepare, beginning in 9th grade. Others specialize in writing the essay or prepping for an interview. And, of course, there are SAT prep courses galore.

With the push on at younger and younger ages, we're paying the price, parents and kids alike. How do you cope with the madness? Let's begin with a look at what stress is, some warning signs of stress overload, and the role you play along the way.

## 1. What are the most common areas of stress among teens?

\* For starters, the "college process" goes on for years, with agony over course selection, grades, SATS, applications, volunteer and extracurricular activities. This process has become a j.o.b.

\* Social relationships are always changing. Today's BFF is tomorrow's enemy. There is pressure to conform, the agony of being excluded, and the temptations of drugs, alcohol, and sex.

\* For girls, more than for boys, body image is a big factor. They are too fat or too thin, too tall or too short. Their skin is a mess (they think), their hair is never right, and someone always has nicer clothes.

## 2. What is stress? Is there good stress, too?

\* Stress is the body's reaction to a real or perceived uncomfortable or dangerous situation. The body reacts by releasing hormones (adrenalin is one) that activate the fight or flight response. All systems are on alert.

\* Yes, there is good stress. It's normal, and has us performing at higher levels. Examples are public speaking, preparing to go to a party, and taking the foul shot that could win or lose a game. When the event is over, the hormones return to normal.

\* Then there is **stress overload**. This is ongoing, low- or hi-level stress such as changing schools, divorce, a death in the family or bullying. It can feel like a constant state of anxiety.

### 3. How do teens respond to normal stress and stress overload?

\* You already know that it shows up in their moods (both boys and girls). Your teen can be impatient, irritable, sad, depressed, anxious and overwhelmed. They will often take it out on family and friends.

\* Physical symptoms include stomach/headaches, allergic reactions such as hives, changes in eating, sleeping and hygiene.

\* Then there are real danger signs: self-abuse (eating disorders, cutting) and abusing drugs and alcohol. They become secretive. This is what happens when they don't know any other way to cope.

### 4. Why does stress increase during the college prep process?

\* With all the pressure, teens feel that today's choices are forever choices. "What if I choose wrong? What if I make a mistake?"

\* There is the stress of maintaining grades and getting into the "best" college.

\* This is a long, drawn-out process, with lots of waiting. Life revolves around college for more years than it should.

### 5. How do parents add to the stress during college prep?

\* With love and concern and the best intentions, parents add to the pressure. You may be micromanaging around grades, homework and extracurricular activities.

\* Parents nag about studying, prepping for the SAT/ACT, completing applications, and may compare their kids to others.

\* You may be complaining (loudly worrying) about the pressures of financing the college education. (Here's where you can set some parameters about the schools to which your child applies.)

Start paying attention to behavior changes that may indicate stress overload. Take a look at your own behaviors and responses when the subject of college comes up. There are always opportunities to take the angst out of the apps.

## Chapter 30

# What to do When Your Spouse Says: "I'm Outta Here!"

### By Carolyn N. Daly, Esq.

Your spouse has announced that they want a divorce. First, don't panic and, although you inevitably will from time to time, try not to react out of emotion. Take some time and digest what you just heard. Then, make sure that there really will be a divorce. Talk to your spouse, if you can; see a qualified therapist, if necessary. People are often shocked to hear a divorce lawyer say that, but going through the process of divorce, and remember it is a process, can be time consuming, emotionally difficult and financially draining. Therefore, you want to be sure it is the right decision.

If your spouse has moved out of the house with little or no warning and cleared out your bank accounts, or taken the children with them, then you may not have the luxury of considering your options and should get to an attorney quickly. However, if there is no rush and the two of you have some time to consider the decision, then the following are some things that you should or should not do to afford you some protection while the decision is being made:

1. Consult with an attorney. You do not necessarily have to retain one at this point, but it is good to have a consultation so that you know what your options are. This is often the best money spent in a divorce.

2. Do not incur any additional debt. Do not sign a home equity loan. Do not sign any business loans. Do not plan any extravagant vacations for which you will go into debt.

3. Do not enter into a contract to buy a new house.

4. Do not sign anything else at the request of your spouse. Review it with an attorney first.

5. Do not liquidate any large assets.

6. If you are not in the habit, start making copies of financial records.

7. If the family finances are maintained on Quicken or a similar personal finance computer program, either print out the records or make a digital copy.

8. Establish credit in your own name. It is easier to obtain credit in your own name prior to a divorce being filed.

9. If you have received any inheritance or gift (other than from your spouse), do not commingle it with marital monies. Keep it segregated and intact. You may need it in the event of separation.

10. Open an account in your own name in a bank where you do not have jointly held accounts and where neither of you does business. It may be advisable to withdraw half the funds from joint liquid accounts, i.e. bank accounts, and to deposit them in an account you hold in your own name, understanding you are fully accountable for the removal of such funds. You may also need to set aside monies for

emergencies and to have funds available for such things as retainers to attorneys, expert's fees, etc.

11. Start keeping track of relevant events, including absences from the home by the spouse, yourself and/or exercise of parenting time/visitation, if applicable. Record dates, times and explanations.

12. Make sure your automobile is in good working condition and has serviceable tires. You should also check the title to see that it is titled in your name or joint names.

13. Undergo necessary medical treatments, so long as they are covered under medical insurance.

14. Keep a low profile. Do not get into verbal or physical altercations. Walk away if necessary.

Once there has been a decision made to divorce, the next question is how to proceed. If you and your spouse are on speaking terms and fairly amicable, then you should consider mediation. Mediation is a process by which you and your spouse meet with a trained, neutral professional, typically a lawyer or mental health professional, to help you resolve all of the issues relating to the divorce. A mediator does not represent either of you, but assists you and your spouse in reaching your own resolution of the issues. It is generally not binding on either of you until a formal agreement is prepared and signed by both of you. Typically parties hire an attorney to advise them during the mediation process. Your attorney can, but is not always required to, attend mediation sessions with you, which can also help keep expenses down. Mediation is often less expensive and less adversarial than traditional divorce litigation, making it attractive to many. However, both of you have to be prepared to communicate and to be cooperative to make mediation effective.

So, mediation sounds good, but having considered it, you determine that it simply will not work for you and your spouse. Before you run to court, there is another option to resolve your issues outside of divorce: arbitration. Arbitration is a process by which you and your spouse agree, essentially, to hire a trained, neutral professional or professionals, to serve as your private judge or judges and decide the issues. Again, an arbitrator doesn't represent either you or your spouse, and the process is conducted much like a trial. Therefore, each of you will probably have hired an attorney to represent you in the process. Witnesses can be called and documents and other evidence produced. The benefit of arbitration is that it typically results in a faster resolution and can be cheaper than traditional litigation. Another benefit is that once the arbitrator has rendered a decision, their decision is final and subject to review by a court under very limited circumstances. This means that you and your spouse will have some finality at the end of the process instead of having to face potential appeals and repeated visits to court in the future.

Another option to resolve your issues without court intervention is collaborative divorce. Collaborative divorce has been around for some time, but has been gaining popularity in many states in recent years. In collaborative divorce, each of you will hire an attorney, but the attorney's role is that of negotiator, not litigator. It is a non-adversarial process and the goal is to reach a settlement. Depending upon the issues and their complexity, you and your attorneys may agree to bring in other professionals, such as accountants, mental health professionals, financial experts, actuaries, etc., to help in resolving the issues. At the start of a collaborative divorce, you and your attorneys agree in writing to exchange all financial and relevant information, which is confidential to the process. This can cut down on the costs of obtaining relevant and necessary documents yourself. It also encourages disclosure of everything by each of you. You and your attorneys also agree in writing, typically in the same document, that should negotiations fail, each party will have to hire a new attorney to litigate the matter, starting from the beginning of the process. The belief is that this requirement keeps the parties focused on a settlement and provides a financial incentive to reaching a resolution.

What happens if none of the above methods to resolve your case will work? Then you are left with resolving the matter in court. You should retain an attorney to represent you. There are many ways to find an attorney. You can ask friends and colleagues for recommendations. You can call your state or local bar and ask if they have a lawyer referral service. You can Google for an attorney. Once you have some names, I suggest that you go for a consultation with some, or all of them, so that you can decide if they are the right fit for you. Do they understand the issues you are facing? Does their view of the case match yours? How do they communicate with you? What are their hourly rates and billing practices? Will the partner be handling your case, or will it be an associate? The list of questions goes on, but it is important that you feel comfortable with the attorney you select to represent you. You should also consider hiring or consulting with an accountant, financial planner or psychologist to help you in resolving the economic and custody issues involved in your case. Your attorney is typically not qualified to provide tax advice, financial advice or mental health advice or support.

Then once you have decided which process is right for you, you need to decide what the issues are between you and your spouse that have to be resolved. In a typical divorce, the following issues are involved:

- Child(ren) custody: Legal and physical, including parenting time and visitation
- Child support; contribution to the children's education, college or private school
- Health and dental insurance for children, including uninsured or unreimbursed medical expenses
- Alimony (spousal support)
- Health insurance for you or your spouse (COBRA)
- Beneficiaries of life insurance policies
- Dividing property – assets and debts
- Marital residence
- Vacation homes, time-shares
- Businesses
- Retirement benefits (pensions, IRAs, 401(k) plans)
- Bank accounts
- Children's accounts – custodial, savings, 529 plans
- Brokerage accounts – stocks, bonds, and funds
- Stock options and restricted stock units

- Cars, boats, motorcycles, RVs, airplanes, etc.
- Home furnishings/collections/jewelry/family photos, etc.
- Airline miles and credit card points
- Debts
- Inheritances
- Tax consequences of the transfers of property pursuant to the settlement
- Tax deductions – i.e., children as dependents, mortgage interest, real estate taxes, etc.
- Domestic violence concerns
- Resumption of maiden name (for women)
- Attorney's fees and expenses

This is certainly not a comprehensive list of the issues that can be involved in resolving your case, but it is a good start. So, now that you know how you are going to resolve your case and what the issues are, what information and documents should you gather to provide to the attorney, or mediator, involved to help resolve these issues? The following is a list of preliminary documents/information that you should gather, bearing in mind that you may not be able to get all of them:

1. Copies of all federal, state and corporate tax returns for the last three years. Have a complete set of each, including all attachments and schedules.

2. A list of all assets (property) and liabilities (debts).

3. For every business involved and for which you or your spouse has access to financial statements, provide the last three fiscal years' financial statements, all year-to-date financial statements, and the same periodic financial statements for the prior year (Quick Books records can be very helpful).

4. Copies of all insurance policies, including life, automobile, medical and umbrella policies.

5. Copies of the most recent statements for all credit cards or a list of all credit cards and obtain one year's statements for these

accounts. If you don't know all of the credit card accounts, obtain a copy of your credit report. You can obtain one free of charge at www.annualcreditreport.com.

6. Copies of statements for all bank accounts for the last year, as well as copies of canceled checks.

7. Copies of statements for children's accounts.

8. A copy of the most recent documents identifying each employment benefit for you and your spouse, i.e., insurances, flexible spending accounts (FSAs), stock options, restricted stock units, etc.

9. Copies of plan documents for all pension plans, 401k plans, profit sharing plans, employee stock purchase plans, etc. Make copies of year end statements (these are usually generated between January and March of each year for every participant in the plan).

10. Copies of statements for all stock accounts and brokerage accounts.

11. Appraisals of property, whether real property or personal property. For personal property, you may have done an appraisal for a rider to your homeowner's insurance.

12. Copies of any loan applications.

13. Copies of financial statements or financial plans prepared by a professional.

14. An inventory of the contents of any jointly held safe deposit box, as well as household valuables such as silver, china, antiques, and art objects. Take pictures of valuable items so that you have a record of them in case they "disappear" before your matter is resolved.

15. A list of return addresses of all mail received by your spouse from brokerage houses, banks, insurance companies, credit cards,

so you can be sure that you didn't miss any assets or debts.

16. Documentation concerning income. For each income source in the current and prior calendar year, including income from employment, investment, government programs, gifts, trust distributions, prizes, and income from every other source, provide pay stubs, a current income statement, and the final income statement for the prior year; e.g., a W-2.

17. Documents that show average monthly expenses for your shelter, transportation and personal expenses, including employment related child care expenses, extracurricular activities, tutors, camps, private education, unreimbursed medical expenses, etc.

Again, this is not an exhaustive list of documents and information that will need to be gathered and provided, but it is a good start. Divorce is a stressful life event, even under the best of circumstances where you and your spouse get along. I hope that this brief overview of the process and things to consider when you are faced with a divorce will alleviate some of the anxiety and provide you with some ways to protect yourself in the event of a divorce.

# Chapter 31

# Divorce Mediation: A Practical Way to Lessen the Costs and Stress

## By Robert McDonnell, MS, APM

Why are so many couples choosing mediation as a means of resolving their separation, divorce, or post-divorce issues?

• *To avoid conflict and the bitterness that comes with these difficult issues* –
With high divorce rates, and very visible celebrity divorce disasters, divorcing couples want to move on with their lives and stay out of court.

• *To save time and money* –
Today's litigated divorces are time consuming and extremely expensive.

• *To focus on the children* –
Most parents agree that the children come first. In mediation, they develop ways to handle joint parenting, but as divorced or

separated parents.

• *To maintain dignity* –
Mediation provides a process that is thoughtful and dignified. It can help parties end a long term marriage with respect.

• *To maintain privacy* –
Parties can keep issues of out court, and financial and custody issues can be resolved in a private setting.

**What is Divorce Mediation?**
Divorce mediation is a confidential and voluntary process where a neutral mediator guides you and your spouse through the negotiation of your separation or divorce in a cooperative, and non-adversarial, setting. The process results in a settlement that becomes the basis for the legally binding divorce agreement. This agreement is typically unsigned by the parties and is called the "Memorandum of Understanding." Because the professional divorce mediator is impartial and unbiased, the process helps parties create a unique separation agreement that works for them as they plan for the future and, if children are involved, as they develop a joint parenting agreement that is in the best interests of the children.

Parties in mediation learn how to recognize and deal with differences, and learn to reach decisions regarding support, equitable division of property, and parenting arrangements. Those using mediation find that they often eliminate the court-imposed requirements and delays, and learn to deal with issues without becoming enemies.

It is generally agreed that divorcing couples are more likely to abide by agreements that they have made themselves, than by court-imposed orders. Mediated agreements have the greater degree of success going forward.

**How Long Does Divorce Mediation Take? How Much Will Mediation Cost?**
Every case is different (of course), but the average divorce mediation might take three to six, one and one-half or two hour

sessions, generally taking a month or two to complete the process. More complex cases can take several months to complete. The cost of the mediator may range from $2,000 to $6,000 in total from both parties for the typical number of sessions. The payment of fees for mediation should be discussed during mediation. The cost for each party's attorney for consulting and review of the agreements is in addition to these mediator costs. Mediation is less expensive than a settlement negotiated by counsel, or a full-blown litigated divorce, either of which can be many multiple times higher than the mediation costs.

## Do I Need a Lawyer During Mediation?

Legal advice is an important part of the mediation process. Mediation is not a substitute for advice of a qualified attorney. Both parties are encouraged to use independent legal counsel for continuing advice during the mediation, and for the legal review of the agreement (the Memorandum of Understanding) before it is signed, or before the attorneys prepare the Divorce Agreement for filing with the court. Legal advice should not come from the impartial mediator. Even when the mediator is an attorney, the mediator cannot give either party legal advice. Although divorcing couples can file court documents on their own, the use of a qualified lawyer is always good advice. Ask the mediator for suggestions for attorneys to help with the legal review and filing requirements.

## My Case is Too Complex for Mediation. What if We Can't Agree on All Issues?

In complicated divorce situations, or with complex financial issues, parties in mediation frequently are advised to consult with outside experts, such as accountants, appraisers, financial planners, and other professionals during the process. The mediator can bring these experts into the process, and include their products and resources in the process.

In cases where the parties agree on all but one or two issues, the time and effort spent in mediation is not wasted. An agreement can be prepared that addresses all of the settled issues, and the parties can then go forward with litigation on the limited issues, or take time to think about the issue(s) and, possibly, return to mediation.

## How Do I Know if Mediation is Right for Us?

If you think that mediation might be something you and your spouse are interested in, but are unsure if it's the right way to proceed, you might consider consulting with a mediator and trying it for a session or two to see how you feel about the experience. Ask questions about the process and your situation, and you should get helpful answers. Most mediators charge on an hourly basis, so this is an inexpensive way to find out about mediation and obtain some information about the process...and the mediator.

## When is Mediation Not Suitable?

There are circumstances where mediation will not be appropriate for your situation. Parties should not participate in mediation where there is a history of emotional or physical abuse, where there is any history of domestic violence or child abuse, or when there is a restraining order in effect. Both parties need to have a sense of self awareness of their individual rights, and not be in a position where they feel forced to agree to terms that would not be in their best interests. For some couples, it may be appropriate to delay mediation until both parties are emotionally ready to participate. An experienced mediator will recognize if you are not ready for mediation and will advise you accordingly.

## How Do I Get Started? Choosing a Mediator.

Couples facing divorce often panic and in the interest of protecting their finances, access to children, or for a myriad of other reasons, turn to litigation as a first step. If you think that mediation might be appropriate for your situation, and you're interested in the benefits of mediation, ask for a referral to a mediator. A good place to start is with referrals from mental health professionals, attorneys, clergy, or others who deal with mediators. Many national and state mediation associations provide useful information, as well as mediator referral services. Internet searching is another effective way to find a local mediator.

Remember, that divorce mediators come from a variety of backgrounds and, in addition to having extensive training and experience in mediation, will have expertise in such fields as mental health, law, business, and accounting, among others. A mediator should have experience and training that is appropriate to your particular situation. You should be comfortable with the mediator and feel that the mediator will be unbiased, open, helpful and capable of assisting you in negotiating your own decisions. A competent mediator should be able to explain and describe the legal requirements in your state for such issues as child support, parenting, equitable distribution, and spousal support. Interview more than one mediator and find one that you both are comfortable working with. Ask about relevant training, experience in handling situations similar to your case, and experience as a mediator and in other professions. Also, ask about fees, how long the process might take and about their resources for experts, as well as attorneys to assist with review of the Memorandum of Agreement.

**Conclusion**
There are many benefits to mediation. Mediation works because you make decisions together. You remain in control of the process, and you avoid the courtroom. The process includes just you, your spouse, and the mediator. Mediation is today's alternative to a contentious divorce. Mediation is the better, easier, and less expensive way to get a divorce. Is it right for you?

## Chapter 32

# I am Not a Victim of Domestic Violence – Speak up & GET OUT!

### By Dr. Tamika Anderson

You're a determined woman: a loving wife and mother, networking, branding with **vision**, and building a great business for yourself. But there is still something missing – your confidence. You know your net worth, but have yet to know your **self-worth** due to the violence and abuse you face at home. You have heard this so many times, but you have always thought it applied to everyone else but you, right? After all, you don't fit the stereotype of the abused woman.

People must more clearly understand the definition and what behavior constitutes abuse.

Domestic violence does not discriminate. It does not matter your race, age, religion, educational level, or your socioeconomic status.

One in four women will be victims of severe violence by an intimate partner during their lifetime. That's approximately five million women per year. On average, <u>three women are murdered everyday</u> by a current or former boyfriend, fiancé, or husband. The Centers for Disease Control reports that since 2003 over 18,000 women have been killed by men in domestic violence disputes.

It took being physically beaten and almost killed in my 20 year relationship and marriage to know that I was being abused. I did not know the warning signs. I knew it did not feel good to be called derogatory names, put down, being told what to wear, and not having money left over. I was completely unaware that verbal, emotional, and financial abuse is a prelude to physical abuse. There are four questions you need to ask yourself to determine if you are a victim of domestic violence:

1. "Does my spouse/intimate partner verbally, physically, or emotionally abuse me?"

2. "Does my spouse control all of the money?"

3. "Does my spouse/intimate partner control where I go or who I spend time with?"

4. "Does my spouse monitor my mail, phone calls, or internet activity?"

If so, you could be the victim of domestic violence.

If any of these examples apply to you, then you very likely are a victim of domestic violence. I recommend that you use my TALK Formula to break the cycle of domestic violence in your life or give it as life – saving advice to a friend.

**T** – Time is of the essence. You need to make up your mind that it's time to get out safely.

**A** – Ask questions. Get on the phone and contact a Domestic Violence Advocate Expert if you believe you are a victim of domestic violence. They can help you create an exit strategy safety plan. One hotline for help is the Domestic Violence and Abuse Hotline: 800-799-7233.

**L** – Listen to your family and friends who are urging you to get out safely. You have to have a plan. A woman is more likely to be killed by her spouse/intimate partner when she is trying to leave or after she has left her abuser.

**K** – Keep your identity safe by having your important documents in one large envelope. These documents may consist of banking information, credit card statements, medical records, passports, etc. Having these documents in one place will assist you if you need to leave in a hurry.

I am passionate about bringing awareness to domestic violence. If any of this is happening to you then please Speak Up & Get Out!

# Chapter 33

# Elder Care: Tough Questions for Your Parents

## By Tracey S. Lawrence, MS
## Founder, Grand Family Planning

Originally published as:
http://traceycaregiver.wordpress.com/2012/09/19/the-toughest-talks-8-things-you-have-to-discuss-with-your-parents/
Updated August 20, 2014.

When you're growing up, one of the toughest things your parents have to summon the guts to address is "the facts of life." Telling your kid about sex is difficult for most folks, and it's not exactly fun for the kids to hear either. Most of us prefer to learn these things from our peers, but many of us receive at least some guidelines and expectations from our parents.

In time, as parents age and kids start noticing their parents' decline, the next tough discussion will have to come up, one way or another. It's far better to start the ball rolling when your parents are still relatively competent and cooperative. Waiting until they're unfit to act on their own behalf is a bad strategy. So it will be left to you to bring up "the facts of age," so to speak.

In most cases, it's unnatural for a child to parent their parents, at least initially. But it happens for most of us, if we're "blessed."

I've had to learn about these things the hard way, so to make your life easier, I have compiled a short list of the things you really need to cover in your tough talk with your parents:

1) Identify all assets: bank accounts, insurance policies, annuities, properties, cars, boats, anything of value with a title attached. Get signature cards signed. Consider joint ownership with rights of survivorship. Catalog everything. There are tools to do this.

2) Insurance: health care & long term care. (Also consider term life policies to cover expenses. A Financial Planner can help with this.) Even if they're eligible for Medicare, it doesn't cover everything. Look into supplemental policies and managed Medicare (AARP has a range of programs called "Secure Horizons" where the insurer gets the money allotted for Medicare and manages the payments and care to minimize out of pocket costs). Long Term Care policies are more affordable when applicants are younger (50 is the sweet spot, 79 is too late) and healthy. There are many different kinds, so work with a professional to learn which might be right for your family.

3) Formal Last Will and Testament. Get these done while your parents are competent to review what they have and sign legal documents.

4) Living Will (advance directives). When would *they* want to pull the plug? It's an extremely important question that needs to be answered formally, in writing, with a lawyer.

5) Durable Power of Attorney: This allows their designee to make decisions and sign papers on their behalf if they can't.

6) Health Care Proxy: Allows their designees to make health-related decisions for them and gets you past the HIPPA red tape.

7) Discuss the Funeral: This really sucks, but you need to find out what they're thinking. In the end, funerals are for the benefit of the living, but you'll be sorry if you don't at least honor what your loved one really wanted. Funeral homes can help you with "pre-

need" assessments; you can pre-arrange and pre-pay (shop around for the right one) and then you only have one number to call on that fateful day.

8) Financial and/or Estate Planning: Make the most of what your parents have left so you can help them to get through the rest of their lives without fear or hardship. And, with any luck, there might even be a little something left for you and your kids. Maybe a pizza party? These days, anything left over is a moral victory.

You may be tempted to put this off indefinitely. Humans tend not to want to confront these difficult issues. If you wait until your parents begin to show signs of dementia, you could be in for a rougher ride. Eventually, we all hit some kind of crisis; that's life. You don't want to be making decisions when you're in that mode. It's easier to make intelligent decisions while everyone is still healthy, so you only have to act upon those decisions when the time comes.

So if you're reading this and thinking it may just be time, IT IS TIME, don't wait. Time marches on, and that's just another inescapable fact of life.

*Please note: This advice is not meant as a substitute for advice from professionals. I encourage you to seek out professional help in making these decisions, for elder care, estate planning, and preparation of the legal documents. Remember, you get what you pay for, and one small error can cost a lot of money; the right pro can save you thousands and can also save lives.*

If you need more information, resources or referrals, please visit LightOfGray.com. I am developing a new organization called **Grand Family Planning**, which will be a club you can join to determine what needs your family has, and will take you step by step through the process of addressing those needs in a manageable, sensible, cost effective way. **Grand Family Planning** is scheduled to launch in January of 2015 and will be serving northern New Jersey.

I hope you'll visit and spread the word.

# Chapter 34

# Medicare and Long Term Care: The Middle Class Crisis

## By Frank R. Campisano, Esq.
### Elder Law Attorney

Jim and Pam are in their early 70s and have steadfastly saved money for their retirement throughout their working life. They are fairly comfortable and are confident that they will have sufficient financial resources to not only see them through retirement, but also to leave their adult children a financial legacy. Then tragedy strikes. Jim suffers a severe stroke which leaves him partially paralyzed and in need of custodial care in an assisted living facility for the remainder of his life. After a few months, the Director of the assisted living facility advises Pam that Medicare will cease covering the cost of Jim's care in two weeks, and that they will have to pay for his care with their own funds. When Pam discovers the cost of Jim's care is $11,000 per month, she declares: "How on earth can we afford this?! Our life savings will be completely wiped out in a few years!"

Unfortunately, Jim and Pam's experience is not unique. Many middle aged and senior citizens are unaware of the staggering costs associated with long-term care in assisted living facilities and nursing homes. Rates for extended stays in such facilities range between $4,000 and $11,000 per month, depending on the level of care required by the resident. Our middle aged and senior population are also tragically unaware that Medicare, which is the primary health insurance for senior citizens, does not cover long-term care costs. Medicare only covers 100 days of treatment in a skilled nursing or sub-acute facility following a hospital stay.

The preferred means for preventing financial devastation caused by long-term care costs is through long-term care insurance, which provides coverage for extended stays in long-term care facilities not covered by Medicare or private health insurance. Long-term care policies, however, are specialized policies that are expensive and therefore unaffordable for many middle class people.

Because of the high costs of long-term care, Medicaid has become the primary means of financing long-term care for the middle class. Medicaid is a federal program administered by the individual states that provides hospitalization and medical benefits for the needy and indigent. Medicaid covers the costs of long term care in nursing homes and assisted living facilities only if the patient's assets and income fall below the federal poverty limit. Most middle class families therefore must pay the staggering costs of long-term care by first exhausting or "spending down" their assets, and then applying for Medicaid.

With advanced planning, Jim and Pam could have prevented their financial devastation. The primary strategy for long-term care asset protection is for families to transfer assets to their children as they approach retirement age, and while they are in a state of good health. The Deficit Reduction Act of 2005, however, imposed a five (5) year restriction on the transfer of assets. Medicaid will deny eligibility and/or impose ineligibility penalties for any transfers made during this five year period.

It is therefore important to start long-term Medicaid planning while both spouses are fairly young and relatively healthy. Transfers to their children can be effectuated through Medicaid compliant trusts that will preserve assets while qualifying for Medicaid long-term care benefits. These trusts, however, are fairly complex and therefore should be prepared by a qualified elder law attorney.

# Chapter 35

# Free At-Home Assistance for Veterans

## By Bonnie Laiderman

There is a very little known program called "aid and attendance" for veterans and their spouses (or surviving spouses). In order for a veteran's spouse to receive the program benefits, the veteran must also be ill. This only for veterans who have served at least 90 days' active duty during World War II, the Korean War, or the Vietnam War. For other wars there are other programs. A secondary qualifier is that you need to have a serious medical condition. The third qualifier is income and assets. The primary formula is that the medical expenses need to exceed income. Home and car are excluded as assets. You do not need to sell off assets, or mortgage your home, to qualify. The goal is to keep people out of a nursing home by providing light housekeeping, laundry, meal preparation, bathing, food shopping, and rides for doctor visits. The maximum number of hours on average for single veterans is 70 hours a month; for a couple, 84 hours a month; and for the surviving spouse, it is 45 hours per month. Also, services can include pairing with the appropriate home nursing services by contracting with companies such as Comfort Keepers.

# Chapter 36

# Government Benefits for Low-Income Individuals

## By Darsi D. Beauchamp, Ph.D.

**TYPES OF MEDICAID**

"Medicaid provides health insurance to parents/caretakers and dependent children, pregnant women, and people who are aged, blind or disabled. These programs pay for hospital services, doctor visits, prescriptions, nursing home care and other healthcare needs, depending on what program a person is eligible for." You must be:

1. A family with children who are dependent on you, OR
2. A person who is 65 years or older, blind, or permanently disabled, OR
3. A woman who is pregnant.

Medicaid can be extremely useful for children with disabilities. The coverage is impressive in that it covers the doctors, therapists, eyeglasses, dental, and medicines the children need, as well as home care and respite. Legal resident immigrants must have been in the United States at least five (5) years before being considered; however, if their children were born here, then they are eligible again depending on income guidelines. Immigration exceptions exist; please refer to the list on the website or simply call or visit your county social services office. Remember that income and assets are taken into consideration and that children are eligible only up to the point they reach their 19th birthday.

## NJ Family Care
This type of Medicaid is for families who are low income and are in need of health care. This health care can have a co-pay, or it can be free. Parents must provide proof of income along with other pertinent documents. Assets are not taken into consideration, just income. The coverage depends on the monthly income and size of the family. The coverage is based on an HMO and applicants will be able to choose the covering company, such as Amerigroup, Horizon Blue Cross and Blue Shield, HealthFirst, and/or United Health Care. The coverage may end for both the parents and the children when the children reach the age of 19 years of age. All applications are available via the online state website, through the mail (in many languages) or by visiting your county social services office. http://www.njfamilycare.org/ index.html

## NJ Kid Care
This is only for children under 19 years of age whose families qualify for free or low cost healthcare services. The services are the same as those for NJ Family Care, except that this type of care has four plans (A, B, C, and D) and is only for the children, not for the parents. Plan A is for low income families whose children qualify at no cost. Plan B is for families with higher income, and Plan C is for families whose income requires a cost share. Plan D is for children whose families have an annual income of up to $58,450 (family of 4), and requires payment of monthly premiums.

## Medically Needy Medicaid
This is for families whose income and assets are too high and exceed the criteria for NJ Family Care or NJ Kid Care. This type of Medicaid allows the family to offset the income by being able to spend down with medical and other care expenses; also, in cases

when a child has a disability and there are typical siblings, then the income can be offset to the typical child in order to help the disabled child qualify. Furthermore, this type of Medicaid may have a monthly premium and/or co-pays. In some cases teenagers who live on their own may be able to apply for themselves; they may be eligible up to age 21.

## Residential Medicaid
This type of Medicaid allows people with disabilities and who are in need of long-term care such as a nursing home and/or any other institution receive services and supports. There is a five (5) year look back provision for eligibility.

## Home and Community Waivers for Medicaid
Waivers Services was created by Congress as a part of the Social Security Act since 1965 to waive some original Medicaid requirements in order to allow individuals with disabilities to receive home and community services and supports to continue to live at home and participate in the community. The waiver Medicaid program may qualify an individual who may not otherwise qualify under the Standard State Medicaid program. There must be a doctor's order, and the person need not be permanently disabled. The supports may include a personal assistant in the home to help with functional situations such as dressing and bathing. Others include vehicle modifications, transportation, case management, day programs, respite, transitional services, and personal emergency response systems.

## AIDS/HIV
This waiver is for people of any age who have AIDS or children up to age 13 who are HIV positive. The services are numerous and also may include placement in a foster home and even reimbursement to DYFS.

## Community Resources for People with Disabilities
This waiver allows the person with disabilities to be able to continue to live in the home and become integrated into the community without having to be bound to an institution.

### Traumatic Brain Injury (TBI)
This waiver allows people who have experienced traumatic brain injuries from ages 21 to 64 to take advantage of the waiver in addition to full Medicaid benefits.

### Community Care
This waiver is for people with disabilities who are registered with the Division of Developmental Disabilities (DDD) and whose disability was manifested before the age of 22 years.

### Long Term Care Global Options
For people 65 years or older or disabled individuals of ages 21 to 64 who are deemed to have a disability by the Social Security Administration, Division of Medical Assistance and Health Services, Disability Review Section. People with chronic mental illnesses and developmental disabilities are not eligible under this category. The services include: "assisted living/adult family care, respite care, home based supportive care, environmental accessibility adaptations, personal emergency response systems, home delivered meal service, caregiver/participant training, social adult day care, special medical equipment and supplies, chore services, care management, transition services and transitional care management, transportation, and attendant care."

### Nursing Facility Transitional Global Options
Same as the long-term care options, but for individuals in a nursing facility that are to transition back into the community.

### Work Options (NJ Work Ability Program)
People with disabilities of ages 16 to 64 can work and earn up to $50,000 a year and not lose their Medicaid benefits. However, they may have to pay a small premium to continue with eligibility.

## SOCIAL SECURITY DISABILITY PROGRAMS

### Supplemental Security Income (SSI)
For children and adults (and those of age 65 or older) who have not worked, individuals who are blind or disabled with limited income and resources. This type of program is nontaxable and has a work incentive available. Your income cannot go over $2,000 a

month to continue to qualify. This plan comes with Medicaid for life.

**Social Security Disability Insurance (SSDI)**
For adults who have worked. This type of program is taxable and has a work incentive available. You can receive it even if you receive worker's compensation. There must be a medical condition or combination of impairment preventing substantial work for at least 12 months or expected to result in death. Determination is based upon age, education, and work experience. To qualify you must have worked 40 quarters of coverage, which equates to 10 years of work. For example, $1,200 of earnings gives you one credit, or 4 quarters a year. If a parent becomes disabled, their child becomes entitled to funds, but entitlement ends at age 19. If a child is disabled, you must file at 16½, and before 19 years of age. Widows and widowers can collect as early as age 50 for their disabled deceased spouses. Social Security Retirement is at 75% if you retire at age 62 (1943-1954), 100% at age 66 (1937-1943), and 132% at age 70 (1960+). Under full retirement, you can earn up to $14,160; over that, you pay $1 for every $2 you earn. At full retirement age, you can earn $37,680; over that, you pay $1 for every $3 you earn; at the month of full retirement, you have no limit on what you can earn annually. Widows and widowers can collect their spouses' social security at age 60 and collect their own at age 66. For more information visit www.socialsecurity.gov

**MEDICARE**
For adults 65 years old or older, or younger with a particular disability (after 24 months of SSDI) or end stage renal disease, Amyotrophic Lateral Sclerosis, Dialysis, and Exposure Environmental Health Hazards (must apply three (3) months before the 65th birthday). This program has a Plan A, B, C, and D. Plan A is hospitalization benefits, Plan B is for outpatient and physician services (this has a premium of about $110.50 a month), Plan C is for Advantage Medicare Plan-Combination of Plan A and Plan B, but with approved private insurance companies. Plan D is the prescription drug coverage. Medicare has co-pays, deductibles, and co-insurance expenses, because of the gap in pay. There is Medigap, a supplemental insurance, as well as others offered by private companies.

**SPECIAL NEEDS TRUST**
Consult an attorney about a special needs trust. However, a special needs trust is necessary in order to allow a person with disabilities to have funds set aside for them. If the funds are in any other type of account, then the person with disabilities may indeed lose their Medicaid and or Supplemental Security Income. Also inquire about how a will may affect a person receiving these government programs.

# Chapter 37

# Understanding Your COBRA Benefits

## By Harry Herbst

When an employee involuntarily loses their health benefit due to being laid off or fired, they are entitled to Consolidated Omnibus Budget Reconciliation Act (COBRA) benefits, which are federally mandated. Employees are eligible for COBRA benefits for 18 months in the state of New Jersey. The employer cannot prevent the employee from signing up and participating in COBRA. Initially, the employee was responsible for the entire COBRA premium. For example, if the premium was $424 per month, the employee had to pay the entire cost. The Obama administration has now implemented a plan called the American Reinvestment and Recovery Act, or ARRA for short. ARRA splits the COBRA premiums between both employee and employer, with the employer paying the bulk of the premium. The employee is now only responsible for 35% of the premium and the other 65% is the employer's responsibility.

Due to ARRA many unemployed former employees are now able

to keep or obtain their group benefits through their former employer. Prior to ARRA many unemployed individuals were responsible for the entire premium and were unable to keep their benefits due to this increased financial burden. Under ARRA the subsidy is allowed for the first nine months of COBRA benefits. After nine months, it then reverts back to the employee being responsible for the entire premium. So for the last nine months of COBRA, the former employee has to pay the entire premium with no discount.

An exception to the COBRA/ARRA rules is for a Survivor Benefit. When a dependent loses their health insurance because a spouse dies, they may remain on COBRA for thirty-six months or three years. These rules apply to someone who is employed in the state of New Jersey, as COBRA rules vary from state to state. If a company closes their doors or goes out of business, all those who have lost their jobs as a result of this, and any former employees previously covered under COBRA, will lose their benefits. Under COBRA law, if there is no business, there are no COBRA benefits.

As a general rule, employers detest COBRA benefits because they don't want to have to collect the premiums from the former employees. If an employee misses a payment or doesn't remit the premium in a timely manner, then the employer has the right to terminate the employee from COBRA, and the employee cannot get back onto COBRA once they have been terminated. Many employers will hire a Third Party Administrator, or "TPA," that will handle the collection of premium dollars and overall administration, maintenance, and reporting that the company would normally have with COBRA participants. It removes the stress of chasing after a former employee from the employer and makes the COBRA process a lot smoother. When an employee voluntarily leaves or resigns from their employer, they are not eligible for ARRA. They are responsible for one-hundred percent of the COBRA premium. When ARRA was created by the Obama administration, it created tax incentives for employers. The employer is allowed to deduct all payments that are made on behalf of the terminated employee.

# Chapter 38

# Understanding Obamacare
# The Affordable Care Act

## By: Harry Herbst

The Affordable Care Act, commonly referred to as Obamacare, passed legislation in September 2013 and was enacted in January 2014. This had an enormous impact on the delivery system for medical benefits for the small business owner as well as individuals. Initially everyone was "traumatized" by the new law, and to some extent still is. As insurance advisors responsible for monitoring group plans, upon seeing premiums increase our initial reaction was that perhaps it should be referred to as the "unaffordable care act." New language and regulations came into effect. For the small business owner, there were "compliance" issues which had to be addressed.

First, a plan consisting of a husband, wife or two business partners was deemed "non-compliant," and the group plan could not be continued unless a third employee was added to the plan. If this could not be accomplished, then the business owner had to establish an individual health medical plan for himself and his family, possibly raising his costs and losing his potential tax deduction. This created an individual burden because an individual policy is not considered a business expense, so is not a tax deductible item for the small business owner. Prior to the Affordable Care Act, family coverage consisted of the business owner, spouse and children as one premium; however, now each individual has their own rate.

Example: the business owner (utilizing a male as an example) has his own rate depending on his age. (New Jersey is an "age rated" state, which means that rate is calculated on the person's attained age. The older an individual, the higher the premium.) The spouse has a separate rate based on his or her own rate.

The children have a separate rate individually for the first three children. If a family has more than three children, any additional child is not charged an additional rate. This new system has caused an increase in premium for the family.

There are six compliance issues which have caused additional challenges for the insurance advisor. As insurance advisors attempting to explain these new regulations, which were a result of the Affordable Care Act, we have been met with disbelief by most business owners.

The small business owner with an existing group coverage must adhere to payroll compliance regulations. For instance, the business owner must provide the insurance carrier proof that the insurance premiums have been continuously paid. This can be accomplished with a WR-30, which is a New Jersey quarterly reporting form to support that everyone is on payroll. (Speak to your insurance advisor for the correct form in your state if you are outside of New Jersey.) If the business owner does not take payroll (which is the instance in many cases), then the business owner needs to provide a K-1 or a W-2 to demonstrate to the insurance carrier that the business owner is indeed the actual business owner and is "legitimate."

# Chapter 39

# Medical Care Discount Plans

## By Ciro J. Giue

The US Bureau of Labor Statistics estimates that 9.1% of the population in the US (or 14 million people) was unemployed at the end of August 2011. It is also estimated that 16.8% of all Americans (or 50.7 million) currently do not have any health insurance. In New Jersey, the figures are 9.4% of the population unemployed (or 421,676 people), and 12.6% (or just over 1 million people) uninsured. Unfortunately, given the poor state of the US and NJ economies, these figures may get worse before they get better. With the rising cost of health care and health care insurance many individuals and families are being forced to choose between going without health care and insurance coverage or putting food on the table. Even if the current health care reform package is enacted as written, many will still go without health care insurance and access to affordable care. Many do not realize that if health care insurance is not affordable to them and their families, they do not have to go without access to quality and affordable medical care for them and their families through a discount plan.

Let me begin by saying that in my opinion there is nothing better than health insurance to protect you and your family in the event of a medical condition. Whether it's a group plan through your employer or a non-group "individual" plan, health insurance typically provides the most robust coverage options for doctor office visits, hospital care, surgeries, medical testing, prescriptions, etc..... The challenge is that many employers are cutting benefits like group health insurance, requiring their employers to pay more of the cost of the premium, and sometimes cancelling group plans completely. Another challenge is that non-group individual health insurance plans in NJ are typically expensive, averaging well over $1,100 per month for the typical family plan. Medical Care Discount Plans enter today's landscape of high unemployment and large groups of uninsured to fill a void and provide access to affordable medical care where health insurance is not an option.

Medical Care Discount Plans in a Nut Shell:

- Provide an affordable alternative to insurance

- ARE NOT INSURANCE

- Participants pay a monthly fee for access to the discount

- Are designed for people who don't have insurance

- Provide a discount at the time the care is provided at participating care providers

- They accept everyone – No restrictions due to age or current/past medical conditions

Sample of Medical Care Benefits These Plans Provide:

- Doctor office visits, including specialists

- Ob/GYN Care

- Dental Care (incl. stand-alone dental plans)

- Vision Care (incl. stand-alone vision plans)

- Prescription Medications
- Radiology
- Hearing Testing
- Chiropractor
- Labs and Diagnostics
- Patient Advocacy

The monthly fee for these plans varies with the level of benefits they offer and usually runs between $19.95 - $79.95 for a single and $29.95 - $120.00 for a family. Specific Coverage Plans are also available for things like Dental and Vision care at cheaper rates ranging from $8/month single and $14/month family.

Discount plans are NOT INSURANCE, so they are not regulated like insurance plans, so buyer beware.

Questions you should ask before you enroll in any Medical Care Discount Plans:

- Is there an application fee?
- Are the fees guaranteed for 1 year or will they change?
- What are the benefits offered?
- Can I see the discounted fee schedule?
- Are there limits to how many times the plan can be used in 1 year?
- Are my current medications covered?
- Are there any monthly administration costs?
- How do I cancel the plan?
- What Care Providers are in your network? (Confirm this with your doctors.)
- Are any care/conditions excluded?
- Whom do I call if I have questions?

These plans are easy to apply for. There is usually a simple, one-page application. They accept everyone regardless of age and/or medical condition. These plans do not have a waiting period and there are no claims/administrative forms; no referral is needed to see a specialist in the Network. So, if insurance is not an option because it is either not available or not affordable, Medical Care Discount Plans can provide an affordable alternative to access quality and affordable medical care.

# Chapter 40

# Frequently Asked Tax Questions

## By Jack M. Bleiberg, CPA

There are some questions that seem to always be asked. I am often surprised that many otherwise knowledgeable people are not aware of the answers, so I took this opportunity to present them. Underlying any tax information is the fact that you are responsible to keep all of your records and receipts for five years, unless fraud is suspected (then, there is no statute of limitations and you will need to prove your assertions). Please also note that each state has nuances of difference from the Federal discussion. For this publication, I am discussing only the Federal considerations, unless stated otherwise. In no way should the contents of this article be considered "tax advice," as that can only be rendered to specific fact sets.

What are Withholding and Estimated Taxes?

Do you sometimes wonder why, at the time of filing your 1040, there may be a large amount due or a refund? When you start a new job and are asked to complete a W-4, do you understand how many exemptions to claim? Withholding and/or estimated tax payments are mechanisms that determine how much tax you prepay for the respective year. You are required, by law, to prepay your taxes throughout the year, or you will be subject to interest and penalty charges. Withholding applies to the classic worker on a company's payroll. Estimates apply to any other significant taxable income and are due in four installments throughout the year, using form 1040-ES. The exemption question on the W-4 allows you to adjust the amount withheld to reflect the tax effects of your spouse and all of your dependents. It is impractical to expand this discussion to include when to claim additional exemptions for itemized deductions, or fewer in the case of other income. I suggest that you consult a tax professional if you suspect that additional exemptions are appropriate.

### Should I consider a ROTH retirement plan (IRA or 401-K)?

A traditional retirement plan allows you to accumulate money that you have not yet been taxed on. However, you pay taxes as the money is withdrawn. In a Roth plan, you accumulate "after tax" money. When you withdraw it, those amounts are tax free. If you believe that your effective tax rate in the current year is less than the tax rate that you will have on retirement, a Roth is for you. For example, if you have earned substantially lower income during the current year that you normally do, consider a Roth. If you are a student, or are just entering the workforce with low earnings, consider a Roth. Bear in mind that current tax rates are the lowest in decades and are expected to be increased in the coming years.

### Are there Retirement Plans for the Sole Proprietor or the Self-employed (and IRA vs. 401-K)?

If you are in your own small business, retirement plan options exist! Even if you are the only person in the company and you are not receiving a paycheck, you may be able to open a "Simple" plan. I always favor the 401-K option. If all goes well economically, the difference is immaterial. However, in hard times, you can borrow up to 50% of your 401-K balance (make sure that the plan is set up to allow it) and pay it back over several years with interest going to your own plan balance. That gives you a huge avenue of relief, should you really need it. You cannot borrow from an IRA.

## What Business Deductions are Available for the Sole Proprietor or Self-employed?

All business related expenses are deductible. Some are subject to limitations. Entertainment and meals are only deducted at 50%. Most significant asset purchases (except land) up to $250,000 per year can be deducted, and the remainder can be claimed as depreciation expense over the useful life of the asset class. Vehicles purchased and leased are subject to special rules. There are limitations based on income and total asset purchases. The IRS has two helpful publications that can be downloaded from www.irs.gov:

- Publication 334 – Tax Guide for Small Business
- Publication 587 – Business Use of Your Home

These are extremely informative and useful. Remember to keep your receipts and, if entertainment, note on the receipt the purpose of the event and who (if anyone) attended.

## Which Types of Business Entity Should I Choose?

This depends on many factors specific to you. In most cases, you should obtain the advice of a tax professional. In order to provide some insight and prepare you for that discussion, these are your choices:

- Unincorporated businesses are businesses for which no formal entity has been established. You are taxed based on the income and expenses as reported on Schedule C of your annual form 1040. The individual is personally responsible for all debts and obligations of the business.

- Partnerships are unincorporated businesses owned by more than one person. A separate form, 1041, must be filed. That form reports the distribution of taxable items between the partners who also receive that information through the schedules K1 of the 1041. The individuals are all personally responsible for all debts and obligations of the business. A Partnership Agreement is required, and a legal name must be approved and registered with the state.

- Limited Partnerships, like partnerships, are unincorporated businesses owned by more than one person. A separate form, 1041, must be filed. That form reports the distribution of taxable items between the partners who also receive that information through the schedules K1 of the 1041. In this case, a class of partners ("Limited Partners") is responsible for the debts and obligations of the limited partnership only to the extent of their investment. There must be at least one "General Partner" who is personally responsible for all debts and obligations of the business. A Partnership Agreement is required, and a legal name must be approved and registered by the state.

- Limited Liability Companies (and Partnerships) are unincorporated businesses owned by one or more persons. If only one person owns it, the income and expenses are reported on the Schedule C of Form 1040. If more than one person owns it, a separate form, 1041, must be filed. That form reports the distribution of taxable items between the partners who also receive that information through the schedule K1 of the 1041. In these entities, all owners are responsible for the debts and obligations of the limited partnership only to the extent of their investment. These are legal entities that must obtain a legal name and must be approved and registered by the state. Written agreements between the owners should be documented.

- Corporations (or "C" Corporations) are the traditional corporation which issues stock. The corporation itself is taxed and files Form 1120. Any distributions to shareholders in the way of dividends are taxed again. The shareholders are responsible for the debts and obligations of the corporation only to the extent of their investment. A Stockholders Agreement is required, and a legal name must be approved and registered by the state.

- Subchapter S (or "S" Corporations) are similar to "C" Corporations, except that the income is not taxed at the corporate level, but flows through to the shareholders. These corporations file annually on form 1120S, the K-1 of which reports the distribution of taxable items between the shareholders. Income is only taxed once. The shareholders are responsible for the debts and obligations of the corporation only to the extent of their investment. A Stockholders Agreement is required, and a legal name must be approved and registered by the state.

# Chapter 41

# I Owe the IRS…Help!

## By Jack M. Bleiberg, CPA

At some point, many taxpayers find themselves in the uncomfortable situation where they owe taxes which they cannot pay when due. Panic sets in. Some people resort to denial and think that they can hide, and just do not file at all. Others get "creative" on their returns and file what might even be a fraudulent return. And, then there are still others that file a correct return and pay what they can at the time. A few write a tearful note in the hope that a kind person will come to their rescue.

Moreover, if you owe money to the IRS, there is an excellent chance that you also owe money on the state level. All states handle this differently. I practice in New Jersey, but the basic advice is the same for all tax authorities. So let's discuss the reactions which I have noted above.

- Yes, it is an awful realization. Bear in mind, that unless you have committed tax fraud, filing a misleading document, or trying to avoid filing altogether (a la Al Capone), the enforcement is financial and you will NOT go to jail. Further, within reason, you will not be forced to live on the street and you will be allowed to buy the basics of life. If you live an extravagant life style and owe a large tax bill, you may be forced to adjust that life style (ask Willie Nelson).

- No, you can no longer hide. The IRS and the states compare information automatically. It is a certainty that if income is reported via W-2, 1099, or similar documentation, all taxing authorities will know about it and compare it to your returns. That being said, you may find that the taxing authorities may not have been able to reconcile similar income originating from multiple sources. In that case, although you may have properly reported income, they will send you a bill. Just reply in writing with a full explanation and they will correct their records.
- Do not get creative by fabricating events (charitable contributions, medical expenses are being scrutinized) that you cannot substantiate. Always report all of your income. Underreporting income is the most serious source of tax fraud.
- If you cannot pay your taxes, do file the return in a timely manner. Given that you cannot successfully hide forever, be aware that there are two levels of penalties. One is late or non-filing, the other is underpayment of taxes. By filing the return, at least you avoid the late filing penalty. By paying a small amount, you can prove that the return was received on a timely basis, as the payment will indicate the date processed. Also, many jurisdictions allow payment by credit card. If your cash shortage is temporary, this may be less expensive than tax interest and penalties. You may even be able to get frequent flyer or similar benefits from the credit card company. You need to compare your credit card rates with the current government rates. If it is even close, pay by credit card. As interest and penalties will continue to accrue each year they are not paid in full, if you owe a very large amount this can happen very easily.

All of this being said, understand that no one is trying to harm you. The agencies are highly automated. Notes attached to the return will not be read or get a response. The underpayment will generate a notice that you did underpay, add interest and a late payment penalty, and include a date that the resulting balance is due. That due date is important to the extent that more interest and penalty will accrue after that date. If you can now pay the tax, pay it. If not, I recommend that you visit the taxpayer assistance center of the IRS or similar state facility. The IRS lists the locations and hours of these centers at http://www.irs.gov/local contacts/index.html. (Be aware that many of these centers close for an unpublicized lunch hour, so call ahead and confirm your timing.) This is where the human being enters the picture. Bring your notice with you and explain your circumstances to the agent. They normally establish a multi-year payment plan with monthly payments. (In some cases, the IRS, has even been known to negotiate forgiveness of a portion of penalties or interest.) This does not stop the interest or penalties from accumulating, but it does stop their collection actions. Check with them, but most of the time this is not reported to credit rating bureaus. It is all very civil and friendly. The key is that you come forward voluntarily and are not trying to avoid paying your taxes altogether. However, you must absolutely be sure that you pay all monthly installments on time, or the arrangement is cancelled and they will aggressively restart collection proceedings, including the possible seizure of your bank accounts. On the other hand, if your financial position improves, pay it off early to avoid the interest and penalties.

If you choose to visit the taxing authority, you do not need to bring your accountant or attorney along with you as long as you speak English and can understand the payment plan as proposed. However, if you are nervous or need an interpreter, then you may want assistance. Typically you are charged for your accountant or attorney's time, so think that through.

Finally, consider what events happened which resulted in your owing such a large balance. You want to correct that situation so that it's not an annual event. Generally, a new payment plan will not be offered unless you do not have an existing plan and have no other taxes owed. If substantially most of your income is from wages or salary, you may not have the proper amounts withheld from your paycheck. It is far easier to have a small part of the tax bill withheld each pay period then to come up with a large payment once a year. Your withholding is based on the form W-4 that you filed with your employer when you were hired. It specifies your marital status and the number of dependents you will claim. If that changes, you need to submit a new W-4. Ask your employer to furnish you with one.

If you have substantial income that is not subject to withholding (business income, interest, dividends, capital gains, pensions, etc.) you may need to pay quarterly estimated tax installments. These forms (1040-ES) are available on the internet, however, I recommend that you see a tax preparer to help you compute the estimate and complete the forms.

In both of the cases of withholding of taxes from pay and the filing of estimated taxes, be aware that these are estimates. The actual tax return will produce the precise tax amount. There will always be at least a small overpayment or underpayment. Depending on your individual situation, you may want to apply all or part of any overpayment to the next year's tax (as an additional estimated tax payment). It is always easier to pay with money that you did not know that you had nor saw in your bank account.

# About the Contributing Authors

## Meet Vivian C. Gaspar

## Vivian Gaspar

800-977-1077
vivian@stopmycrisis.com

Vivian Gaspar is an author, keynote speaker, entrepreneur, and independent business owner of several businesses over the last 25 years. Ms. Gaspar is dedicated to helping her clients survive critical financial times and achieve success.

As the Chief Mortgage Modification Specialist with V. James Castiglia's legal office in New Jersey, she reached out to and worked with over 300 families to help them keep their homes from foreclosure. Ms. Gaspar has given over a hundred key note addresses on mortgage modification, foreclosure mediation, and identity theft prevention at a variety of venues. Some of these venues included The Learning Annex, Department of Labor, various township adult education classes, local libraries, and numerous civic organizations, such as Lions and Rotary clubs.
Ms. Gaspar currently assists business owners in attaining critical

capital and merchant services as a representative of Senape Capital. Senape Capital provides access to emergency and small business funding and merchant services. Ms. Gaspar also provides affordable access to legal services through Legal Shield, a legal services vendor, as well as identity theft protection and restoration. Ms. Gaspar has a wealth of knowledge on managing personal and professional crises from her years of working with individuals and businesses in crisis. Her passion is to share her deep knowledge of navigating crises with the general public through frequent network television and radio appearances in which she speaks on a variety of topics, from entrepreneurship to identity theft. Her recent books, "Stop My Crisis- Facing Life's Challenges Head On" and "Stop My Crisis- Be the 1 in 5" are part of her latest effort to empower people with the diverse information that they need to move past their current crisis into prosperity and successfully follow their dreams.

*Vivian is author of the chapters* **ID Theft & Protection** *and* **Making Money from Home**, *co-author of the chapters* **Mortgage Modification** *and* **Understanding the Foreclosure Process**. *You may reach Vivian through the information below:*

Vivian C. Gaspar
Ph#: (800) 977-1077
url: www.StopMyCrisis.com
email: Vivian@StopMyCrisis.com

## Meet
## Julbert J. Abraham

Julbert J. Abraham has 10 years of experience in Marketing, Sales and Entrepreneurship. He is the CEO of Abraham Global Services, LLC and the Managing Partner of Abraham Global Marketing (AGM). AGM is a marketing boutique located in the Greater New York City area with a focus on LinkedIn Marketing. AGM provides Educational Webinars, Workshops, Courses and Seminars where we teach our clients how to Leverage LinkedIn to grow their Business. In addition, we provide Account Management Services where we support our clients' LinkedIn accounts.

Julbert comes from a humble beginning, born and raised in Port-au-Prince, Haiti. He came to the US at an early age, where he received a Bachelor's Degree in Marketing at Cheyney University in Pennsylvania, then his MBA at Northeastern University in Boston, Massachusetts. In his spare time, he enjoys traveling, cooking, networking and giving back to his community by mentoring the youth and volunteering with local non-profits.

*Julbert is author of the chapter:* **LinkedIN: The Job Seeker's Secret Weapon – 7 Steps to Get a Job on LinkedIn.** *You may reach Julbert through the information below:*

Julbert J. Abraham
AGM – 862-253-1837
www.abrahamglobal.com

## Meet
## Dr. Tamika Anderson

Dr. Tamika Anderson, Connextion Works, LLC; Know Your Worth mentor, coach, and author of ***Speak Up & Get Out!*** was once this woman who suffered in silence. She has worked in the corporate and government sectors, taught undergraduate college students, has over 15 years of experience in the sales, marketing, and service sectors. She also holds a Bachelor of Arts in Psychology, a Master of Science in Organizational Leadership, and a Doctor of Science in Information Systems and Communications.

Dr. Tamika has seen the above scenario play out in the lives of so many women she's encountered while leading her business seminars and workshops. Once Dr. Tamika saw a pattern of low-esteem in the women she consulted with, business became personal. "It **awakened** me inside," says Dr. Tamika. "It's a dirty little secret that must be addressed in order for women to build their worth, get back to business and step into their **true purpose**."

*Transforming lives through purposeful action* is Dr. Tamika's motto, and it's implemented through her five step I.K.N.O.W. system, which also helps with business planning. Her system teaches you how to identify your worth, know the value of your worth, navigate and position yourself to **play a bigger game**, own your message, and wow the world with your worth. There is a process to progress. Dr. Tamika waters the seeds to help her clients grow and maintain their self-confidence.

*Tamika is author of the chapter:* ***I am Not a Victim of Victim of Domestic Violence – Speak Up & Get Out!*** *You can connect with Dr. Tamika A. Anderson at:*

www.TamikaAnderson.com
info@ConneXtionworks.com
@ConnextionWorks

## Meet
## Stephanie Banks

When she was in the eighth grade, Stephanie's father bought her 20 shares of a mutual fund and a copy of the Wall Street Journal, handed it to her and said, "Now you're an investor, start learning." Fast forward eight years – the Biology major who hung out at the Met ended up with a series 6 NASD license selling mutual funds to business owners in SoHo.

After a few years working for a Wall Street Firm, Stephanie took her much desired Series 6 license and settled back in NJ at Equitable Insurance, licensed in Life, Accident and Health insurance. Ever the artist, a few years later she left the financial world to pursue a career in the restaurant industry, working her way up and eventually graduating from the Culinary Institute of America, where she was awarded a graduate fellowship. After many successful years as Executive Chef for corporate clients, Stephanie realized the dream of home ownership and the potential hazards of placing your trust and hard earned money in the hands of lenders who may not have your best interests at heart. Stephanie's financial interest was rekindled as she learned about the mortgage industry and witnessed the unscrupulous behavior of many loan originators. She has been a mortgage consultant for six years, and has worked for both mortgage brokers and bankers. She entered the industry when it was commonplace to receive daily emails announcing the beginning of the end for many lenders.

Her passion is client education. She feels that in order for there to be a successful, long term client/trusted advisor relationship, both loan officer and client education is necessary. "There are too many people that have mortgages whose only purpose was to line the pockets of uncaring, bad loan officers. People need to have faith and trust in the lending system again." Stephanie lives in Southern New Jersey with her husband and daughter and their two dogs. She spent six active years as a leader in the Girl Scouts and is a member of her church choir. She is also a musician in piano, organ and voice in area churches.

*Stephanie is the author of the chapter:* **Understanding Mortgages**. *You may reach Stephanie through the information below:*

Stephanie M. Banks
Loan Originator  NMLS #324908
3110 Chino Ave. Ste. 290, Chino Hills, CA 91709
C: 609-694-7936
sbanks@afncorp.com
www.afncorp.com

# Meet
# Darsi D. Beauchamp, Ph.D.

Dr. Darsi D. Beauchamp has had extensive training in the area of education and administration. She holds a Bachelor's in Psychology and one in Spanish/French from Rutgers University, with certifications in both New Jersey and California to teach grades Pre-K-12, as well as a Master's in Counseling (Family Therapy focus) from California Polytechnic and another Master's in Educational Administration/Business Administration from Montclair University. In addition, she has a doctorate (Ph.D.) in Educational Administration from Capella University in Minnesota, which she has used in managing schools, companies, and government agencies in the private and public sectors. Furthermore, she has years of experience in the areas of marketing, human resources/employment law, counseling, teaching, and translations. She is fluent, bilingual, and biliterate in Spanish, and conversant in French. Her Behavior Analysis Certification is from Saint Joseph's University in Philadelphia.

Some of her employment opportunities, and her doctoral program, have allowed her to be involved in the development of curriculum in differentiated instruction to help all students (Pre-K-College and private companies) in the area of learning interdisciplinary comprehensive studies. Her philosophy is that "all students have the ability to learn, given the right opportunity, skills, strategies, and environment." She has trained many teachers in this methodology and in supervision and is a Staff Development Provider with the New Jersey Department of Education.

Her dissertation was published in the Journal of Biology, Neurology and Education for her contributions in how the brain learns and interacts with the environment, thus promoting lessons that tap into the children's curiosity by holding their attention while using all their senses in learning, taking into consideration their learning needs and pace. Recently, she has changed careers and delved into the area of law by becoming a Paralegal (Fairleigh Dickinson University, Madison, NJ), and is working with different agencies in the areas of disabilities and employment law. Her goal is to go on to law school to continue her contributions in school and employment law. She is also a court-appointed mediator trained by the New Jersey Association of Professional Mediators (NJAPM) and a non-attorney advocate.

She is a member of the American Association of University Women, New Jersey Association of Women Business Owners, NJ State Chamber of Commerce, Latin-Vision, Hispanic Chamber of Commerce, Alpha Epsilon Lambda, National Association of Elementary School Principals, National Association of Judiciary Interpreters and Translators, New Jersey Association of Paralegals, Universidad de Salamanca, Association for Supervision and Curriculum Development, NJ Special Education Providers, New Jersey Association of Professional Mediators, and the American Red Cross.

*Darsi is author of the following chapters:* ***Get Educated for Low to No Cost, Get Special Education Help for Students with Disabilities at No Cost****, and* ***Government Benefits for Low Income Individuals****. You may reach Darsi through the information below:*

Advanced Learning and DDB Productions
P.O. Box 302
Morris Plains, New Jersey
dbeauch@optonline.net
973-400-9794

## Meet
## Jack M. Bleiberg, CPA

Jack is a practicing CPA who has a developed proficiency in guiding companies to reach their full potential through proper planning and execution, and maximizing operational efficiency and controls. He also works with his clients to protect their wealth with proper tax, business exit and estate planning. Jack has worked with all sizes of entities, from small through large public companies.

Jack has been a partner at a regional CPA firm, and owned and operated business systems and consulting firms. Jack has over twenty-five years of experience owning and operating small businesses. He has extensive experience across many industries.

Jack is a graduate of Lehigh University, where he obtained a Bachelor's degree in Accounting He has been published in the CPA Journal and chaired a committee of the NJ Society of CPAs. Jack is currently Vice President and Executive Board Member at the Daughters of Israel Geriatric Center in West Orange, NJ. He is a member of the American Institute of CPAs, the NJ Society of CPAs, and is active with the North Essex Chamber of Commerce.

*Jack is the author of the chapters:* ***I Owe the IRS...Help!****, and* ***Frequently Asked Tax Questions.*** *You may reach Jack through the information below:*

Email: Jack@JBleibergCPA.com

Website: www.JBleibergCPA.com

## Meet
## Santo Bonanno, Esq.

No Picture Available

Mr. Bonanno was born in New Jersey, and completed 9 years of military academy education.

He graduated from the University of Bridgeport School of Law in 1980, receiving his Juris Doctor, and was admitted to the Connecticut Bar Association that same year. He was admitted to the New Jersey Bar Association in 1981. In 1989, he was admitted to the New York Bar Association.

BANKRUPTCY PRACTICE
Creditors' rights and bankruptcy related litigation
Chapter 7, liquidation cases
Chapter 11 and Chapter 13 reorganization cases

Mr. Bonanno has a wealth of experience in variety of civil actions in both federal and state courts as well as corporate and auditing experience, including a successful defense of prevailing wage before the NJ Supreme Court.

His education, B.S. in Accounting and M.S. in Taxation, and his work experience prior to going into private practice are most beneficial when handling corporate, commercial and bankruptcy matters. Mr. Bonanno worked as an IRS auditor and as an auditor for the State of Connecticut. Additionally, he was employed as a tax accountant for Richardson Merrill (a pharmaceutical company), and a tax manager and corporate counsel for Lonza, Inc. (a chemical company). While residing in Franklin Lakes, NJ, for eighteen years, for thirteen years he served as a member of the Board of Education, including two terms as President of the Board. Additionally, he served on the Blue Ribbon Mayor's council committee and coached soccer for the Recreation Commission.

*Santo is author of the chapter:* **Bankruptcy Basics.** *You may reach Santo through the information below:*

SANTO J. BONANNO, Esq.,
Attorney and Counselor at Law
1430 Route 23 North Wayne, NJ 07470
Tel: (973) 686-9060 Fax: (973) 686-9062
santobonanno@optonline.net

## Meet Frank R. Campisano, Esq.

**Elder Law Attorney, Estate Planning Specialist**
Partner – Sedita, Campisano, & Campisano, LLC

Frank R. Campisano is an experienced New Jersey elder law attorney. His passion for helping families and the elderly is real and reflected in his compassionate approach and his above and beyond commitment to his clients. He assists families with estate planning, will and trust administration, and every area of elder law planning and preparation.

This includes issues such as marital shelter trusts, life insurance trusts, generation-skipping trusts and Family Limited Partnerships. He also specializes in Medicaid asset protection and planning, VA

Aid & Attendance benefits, guardianships, special needs trusts, and estate and trust planning, design and litigation.

Mr. Campisano is admitted to practice in New Jersey. He is also admitted to practice before the U.S. District Court for the District of New Jersey, the U.S. District Courts for the Southern and Eastern Districts of New York, the United States Court of Appeals, 3rd. Circuit and the U.S. Supreme Court.

Specialties: Estate planning, will and trust administration, Medicaid planning, guardianships, and estate and trust litigation.

**Education**
Seton Hall University, B.A., 1978
Rutgers University, M.S., 1981
Widener University, J.D., 1983

**Professional memberships**
- New Jersey State Bar Association

Member: Labor and Employment Section

*Mr. Campisano is author of the chapter:* **Medicare and Long Term Care: The Middle Class Crisis.**

## Meet
## V. James Castiglia, Esq.

Jim Castiglia graduated from Montclair Academy in 1970 and earned his Bachelor of Arts degree from Dickinson College, Carlisle, PA in 1974. He also had the privilege of studying for a year at the College's Center for European Studies at the University of Bologna, Italy. He earned his Doctor of Laws degree from Seton Hall University School of Law in 1977. He has been in private practice his entire career, first in West Orange, NJ, and for the last 19 years in Oak Ridge, NJ (Morris Co.).

Jim's practice focuses on individual, family and small business legal needs. He is particularly experienced in residential and commercial real estate. He began doing loan modifications before the government's HAMP program was announced and has always processed loan modifications in-house. He helps people in foreclosure by representing them at foreclosure mediation hearings and uses the hearings as a means to obtain a loan modification. In the last several years a large part of his real estate practice has been mortgage modification negation, foreclosure prevention through mediation hearing, as well as the quick disposition of short sales, both for the Buyer and the Seller.

He is active in his local Jefferson Township Rotary club and is active in the national leadership of his college fraternity, Alpha Chi

Rho.

He has three college-aged children.

*James is co-author of the chapters on* **Mortgage Modification**, *and* **Understanding the Foreclosure Process.** *You may reach James through the information below:*


V. JAMES CASTIGLIA
A Professional Corporation
 Counsellor At Law
5701 Berkshire Valley Road
Oak Ridge , NJ , 07438

Phone:     973-697-1676
Fax:          973-697-1053
Email:      vjc@vjamescastiglia.com

## Meet Brian Cody, CFP

## BRIAN CODY, FINANCIAL ADVISOR

Brian Cody, CFP®, is a Financial Advisor with LPL Financial. Mr. Cody specializes in all phases of financial planning with an emphasis on Retirement Planning for small businesses and individuals. His practice is located out of Florham Park, NJ.

Mr. Cody graduated from the United States Merchant Marine Academy in Kings Point, NY and has a Master's Degree from Union College in Schenectady, NY. Mr. Cody is fully registered for securities and licensed for insurance services.

Brian is also licensed by the State of New Jersey to provide Continuing Education to Certified Public Accountants.

Mr. Cody provides financial presentations to groups around the New Jersey/New York area and is an Adjunct Professor at

Fairleigh Dickinson University in Madison, NJ.

A little known fact about Brian is that after graduating from the US Merchant Marine Academy, he became a US Navy Nuclear Engineer and trained Navy officers to become licensed nuclear engineers.

*Brian is author of the chapters:* **Finding the Right Financial Advisor**, *and* **Should I Pay Off My Mortgage Early?** *You may reach Brian through the information below:*

    Brian T. Cody

    CERTIFIED FINANCIAL PLANNER™

    LPL Financial*
    30 Vreeland Road, Building A
    Suite 120
    Florham Park, NJ 07932
    brian.cody@lpl.com
    Phone: 973-867-1345
    Fax: 973-490-6429

    *Member FINRA/SIPC

Vivian C. Gaspar

## Meet Terrence Coughlin, CPCU, ARM, AIC

Terrence P. Coughlin is a professional Insurance and Risk Management Consultant with nearly thirty years of finance and insurance experience. He is the principle of Task Risk Management Consulting, Inc, located in Wyckoff, NJ. He has held senior positions in the finance and insurance brokerage arenas before spending the last ten years as a Risk Management Consultant.

In addition to his hands-on experience, Terrence has also worked hard on the technical/academic side; earning the Charter Property and Casualty Underwriter (CPCU) designation, which is the most advanced designation in the insurance industry.
In addition to earning his CPCU, he has also earned his Associate in Risk Management (ARM) and Associate in Claims (AIC) Designations.

Terry Coughlin continues to keep up-to-date on his insurance knowledge by teaching CPCU and ARM courses on a regular basis. He is also a member of the Society of Risk Management Consultants (SRMC) and is a Past President of the New Jersey Chapter of the CPCU Society.

*Terrence is the author of the chapter:* **Financially Surviving Natural Disasters**. *You may reach Terrence through the information below:*

Task Risk Management Consulting, Inc.
Terrence P. Coughlin, President
CPCU, ARM, AIC
245 Braen Ave, Suite F
Wyckoff, NJ 07417
(201) 425.8363 Office
(201) 425.8398 Fax
coughlin@taskrmc.com email
taskrmc.com website

## Meet
## Carolyn N. Daly, Esq.

Carolyn N. Daly, Esq., is a partner of Daly & Associates, LLC (www.dalyfamilylaw.net) in Morristown, New Jersey. She is a Certified Matrimonial Law Attorney and has been named a Super Lawyers, Rising Star from 2006 through 2010.*

Her prominent practice focuses on family law (divorce, alimony, college contribution, domestic violence, mediation, custody, parenting time, grandparents' rights, non-dissolution) and real estate law.

Ms. Daly prides herself on a pragmatic, no-nonsense approach to resolving family law matters. She has a diverse background, focusing on family law after having practiced in several other areas, which helps her identify issues that are often overlooked. An active member of the New Jersey State, Morris County, and American Bar Associations, Ms. Daly sits on the Morris County Child Support Partnership Committee. She regularly serves as an Early Settlement Panelist in Morris County.

*Carolyn is the author of the chapter:* **What to do When Your Spouse Says: "I'm Outta Here!"** *You may reach Carolyn through the information below:*

16 South Street
Second Floor
Morristown, NJ 07960

Telephone: 973-292-9222
Facsimile: 973-933-0099

## Meet Ciro J. Giue

**Mission Statement:** *"Great employees make companies. I help great companies keep and attract great employees by helping them design and implement great employee benefits programs that protect their employees and their families & help protect their bottom line."*

Mr. Giué has spent the past seven years consulting with individuals, families, business owners & employers on personal insurance matters and designing effective and affordable employee benefits, health, and welfare programs. Because of Mr. Giué's background as a CPA in NJ, he has experience advising his clients & their employees on designing and implementing sophisticated Group Health & Welfare Plans including IRC Section 105 Plans, IRC Section 125 Plans, High Deductible Health Plans, Flexible Spending Accounts, Ancillary Group Benefits, and Voluntary Supplement Benefits. Prior to this Mr. Giué spent 15 years on Wall Street working in various capacities for a firm that managed assets for institutions, foundations & families. His roles on Wall Street included Compliance Officer, Assistant Treasurer of Mutual Funds, and Investment Reporting Manager. Prior to working on Wall Street Mr. Giué worked as a CPA for the largest CPA firm headquartered in NJ.

## Qualifications

- MBA – Finance/International Business, New York University, Leonard N. Stern School
- Bachelor of Science – Accounting, Rutgers University
- Life and Health Insurance License – NJ, NY, PA, Conn.
- FINRA Series 7 and Series 66 License
- Successful completion of the Long Term Care Planning Master Class
- Certified Public Accountant – License is inactive in New Jersey Associations & Memberships

## Community Involvement & Interests

- Recipient of the Boys & Girls Clubs of America Service To Youth Award
- Founding Member – MSO Prosperity Chapter of Business Network International
- Bilingual – English and Italian (Communicable in Spanish)

*Ciro is the author of the chapter:* **Medical Care Discount Plans.** *You may reach Ciro through the information below:*

**Ciro J. Giué, MBA**
**Chief Protection Officer / Chief Benefits Officer**
Kinnelon, New Jersey 07405
(201)694-3742 - cjgiue@aol.com

## Meet Harry Herbst

Mr. Herbst is a licensed insurance agent who started in 1975. He started his own Insurance Agency in 2002 working with small business owners in the small employee benefits arena. Mr. Herbst is a member of the National Association of Insurance agents and Financial Advisors NAIFA. He is also a member of the National Association of Health Underwriters (NAHU) and was awarded a membership to the prestigious Million Dollar Round Table (MDRT.)

Mr. Herbst also proudly served his country as a US Navy Veteran. He is also Senior Vice Commander of the Jewish War Veterans and a Trustee of Freehold Jewish Center. He has also been active in the various Networking Associations and Chambers of Commerce.

Mr. Herbst holds a BA from the City University of New York and has an MA from the New School for Social Research.

*Harry is the author of the chapters:* **Understanding Your COBRA Benefits**, *and* **Understanding Obamacare**. *You may reach Harry through the information below:*

HARRY HERBST & ASSOCIATES
Insurance & Financial Planning
708 Ginesi Drive
Suite 206
Morganville, NJ 07751
(732) 536-5200
(732) 536-5201 (Fax)
1-888-786-5201 (toll free)

Vivian C. Gaspar

## Meet
## Bonnie Laiderman

Bonnie Laiderman has a broad range of professional experience that spans several decades in the medical care industry and general business. She began her career as payables supervisor at Jewish Hospital in St. Louis, and quickly was promoted to billing manger, responsible for over $100 million in receivables and nearly two dozen employees. She then became credit manager and was responsible for all collections for the hospital. She opened an automotive import/export business, which she owned for 18 years. The company garnered recognition that included the Governor's Exporter of the Year Award and 1998 Exporter of the Year. In 2003, Bonnie founded Veterans Home Care.

The idea for Veterans Home Care came to Bonnie after the passing of her own mother, Edith Sperling, the widow of a Korean War veteran. Bonnie discovered late in Edith's battle with cancer, that a little-known Veterans Administration pension existed to help pay for home care for veterans or their surviving spouses. Unfortunately, by the time Bonnie was able to apply for the pension on Edith's behalf, it was too late. Bonnie realized that many veterans or spouses were not aware of, or were unable to apply for the pension without assistance. Within a few months of Edith's death, Bonnie opened Veterans Home Care to help deserving veterans obtain the pension.

Veterans Home Care helps veterans and their surviving spouses who qualify, apply for a pension, known as "Aid & Attendance," which pays for assistance with activities of daily living in their homes. Veterans Home Care provides home care, assigns attendant care workers and follows up to assure that the veteran remains in compliance with VA guidelines to continue receiving the pension. There are no out-of-pocket costs to the client; VHC furnishes a zero-interest loan for the cost of home care until the application is approved and VA reimbursements begin. Veterans Home Care has helped more than 3,500 veterans or their surviving spouses to access VA benefits for the care they need. The company currently maintains 11 offices, serving clients in 15 states. The company has been recognized by Inc.5000 as one of America's fastest growing companies for 2009 and 2010, and is Better Business Bureau accredited. Bonnie also serves on the board of ITNAmerica (Independent Transportation Network), an organization which provides low-cost transportation to elderly who can no longer drive.

*Bonnie is the author of the chapter:* **Free At-Home Assistance for Veterans**. *You may reach Bonnie through the information below:*

bonnie@veteranshomecare.com
Veterans Home Care
11861 Westline Industrial Drive, Suite 750
St. Louis, MO 63146
314.514.2444 office
800.640.7988 fax
www.veteranshomecare.com

## Meet
## Tracey S. Lawrence

Tracey Lawrence is a woman of many talents. For years, she ran her own graphic arts business. She earned a Master of Science in digital imaging and design from New York University in 2007, endowing her with video editing, animation and broadcast design skills. She uses that knowledge to run Ringwood NJ's public access TV station. Caregiving her aging parents presented challenges for Tracey as she tried to continue running and growing her business. The changing economy didn't help. But as more friends and acquaintances had questions for her about their aging parents, Tracey realized her expertise with elder care was sorely needed. Having been a client of Ameriprise Financial since 2001, Tracey understood the value of working with professionals, and thought she might be able to help more people by becoming an advisor herself. She applied for a position in Ameriprise Financial's Targeted Career Changer program and was hired in March of 2013. After going through a rigorous five month program, she studied for and received her Series 7, Series 66 and Life and Health Insurance licenses. Through her journey, Tracey forged relationships with professionals in complementary businesses, and came up with the idea for "Grand Family Planning:" addressing the needs of multi-generational families, from grandparents to grandkids, helping them to plan for and cope with life's challenges. Working with strategic partners, she provides education, needs analysis and action plans for families in order to live healthier, more secure lives. Tracey is also the lead singer for a New Jersey rock band called "Cozmopolitanz." You can see performances of her previous band, Just Play! on their web site: http://justplayrockband.wordpress.com.

*Tracey is the author of the chapter:* **Elder Care: Tough Questions for Your Parents**.

## Meet
## Joanne Lucas

Joanne Lucas is Manager of Staffing, Winston Staffing, in Rutherford, NJ. Ms. Lucas has been a recruiter for over 25 years. She started before fax machines were even a figment of someone's imagination and now job seekers wouldn't think of working without the Internet!

Ms. Lucas is on advisory boards of post high school educational facilities where she helps place their students, as well as aiding in preparing them for interviews and the workplace. Ms. Lucas has assisted in interviewing students who are applying for scholarships and worked to recommend the winners.

Ms. Lucas especially likes helping candidates take the next step in their careers. She helps determine the social and educational life of the people that we work with, as well as aiding our clients grow their businesses.

Ms. Lucas specializes in Education and Real Estate, but also work with opportunities in the Administrative areas.

Ms. Lucas is married to John De Silva; her daughter, Suzie, is married and is a music teacher on an Indian Reservation in Arizona.

*Joanne is the author of the chapters:* **Acing Your Next Job Interview**, **The Right Answers for Those Tricky Interview Questions**, **and How to Get Your Recruiter to Focus on You**. *You may reach Joanne through the information below:*

Joanne Lucas
Manager of Staffing
301 Route 17 North
Rutherford, NJ 07070
201-460-9200x204
jlucas@winstonstaffing.com
www. winstonstaffing.com

## Meet
## Robert J. McDonnell, MS APM

Robert J. McDonnell, owner and principal of Alliance Mediation Services, has been formally practicing mediation since 2003 and brings to his practice over thirty years of experience in the telecommunication industry, focused primarily on regulatory policy development and issue resolution.

He served as President – New Jersey Association of Professional Mediators (NJAPM), from October 2008 through September 2010. He currently serves on the NJAPM Board as Immediate Past President.

Robert is an Accredited Professional Mediator (APM) and received accreditation from the New Jersey Association of Professional Mediators. His practice includes both civil and family mediation services in New Jersey. He has also been accredited as an Advanced Mediator Practitioner by the Association of Conflict Resolution. Robert was trained in mediation and dispute resolution at Rutgers University, where he received a Graduate Certificate in Conflict Management. He holds a Master of Science degree in Engineering Management and a Bachelor of Science in Electrical Engineering, and also attended graduate policy programs at

Stanford and the University of Michigan.

Robert is approved by the New Jersey Administrative Office of the Courts (AOC) for the Presumptive Mediation Program for Civil, General Equity and Probate Cases and mediates civil cases for the AOC in several counties in Northern New Jersey. He is also on the New Jersey AOC Roster of Foreclosure Mediators. He volunteers his mediation services and serves as a mediator for the municipal courts in Essex, Morris and Passaic Counties.

He is also an arbitrator, and participates on the Financial Industry Regulatory Authority (FINRA) panels in New York and New Jersey.

*Robert is the author of the chapter:* **Divorce Mediation: A Practical Way to Lessen the Costs and Stress**. *You may reach Robert through the information below:*

Robert J. McDonnell, MS APM
Accredited Professional Mediator
Alliance Mediation Services
39 Alpine Drive
P.O. Box 87
Lincoln Park, NJ 07035-0087
Tel: 973 709-0188
Fax: 973 709-0255
rmcdonnell@alliance-mediation.com
www.alliance-mediation.com

## Meet
## Michael Menihan

As a seasoned business expert with 37 years in the Telecommunications Industry, Mike has managed various organizations at AT&T during the Telecommunications Deregulation era, in the 1980s and 1990s.

Mike has also managed various organizations at Emerald Solutions, Inc. and Global Crossing, LLC. Mike has been a small business owner from 2001 to the present. He entered the energy market in early 2010, and currently holds the position of National Consultant with America Approved Energy Service Direct.

*Mike is the author of the chapter:* **Save On Your Energy Bills.** *You may reach Mike through the information below:*

Mike Menihan
America Approved Energy Service Direct
National Consultant
Phone: 973-998-4062
Email: mike.voltage@gmail.com
Website: www.volt.ichoosesavings.com

## Meet Peter Nagy

Peter is a reverse mortgage professional who truly enjoys working with seniors and changing their lives for the better.

The most successful reverse mortgage professionals treat the category as their main line of business, not a sideline. Peter is dedicated to stay abreast of the latest developments in the mortgage industry, which undergoes constant change in their guidelines and regulations. It takes a special kind of person to truly excel in the reverse mortgage business which involves educating prospective senior clients, and allowing them to take all the time they need to make a decision they're comfortable with.

Peter is a graduate of American University in Washington, DC where he obtained a Bachelor's degree in marketing and finance. He is also a Certified Credit Consultant and speaks nationally to mortgage brokers/bankers, real estate agents and financial professionals about how to help their client's achieve the credit scores they truly deserve.

Peter states that, "I really enjoy the business of mortgage banking because I have the opportunity to consult my clients with regard to a major financial transaction in their life. Ultimately, they are grateful when I put them into a mortgage program that not only fits their needs but also their budget. As a trusted advisor, I take great pride in knowing that I am doing what's in the best interest of my clients."

*Peter is the author of the chapter:* **Reverse Mortgages: A Financial Option for Seniors.** *You may reach Peter through the information below:*

Peter Nagy
Licensed Mortgage Originator
NMLM 207869
973-985-1680

## Meet Frances Pepe

Frances M. Pepe
Born and raised in NJ; mother of four

BS – Business (Accounting, Education)
MA – Administration, Supervision & Finance

Broker/Owner
1 Real Estate Network
Peak Estate Associate & Broker since 1984
Owner of Tax One Plus, PTRP
IRS Certified Professional Tax Preparer
Adjunct at Dover Business College and Berkeley College

*Frances is the author of the chapter:* **The Real Estate Buying Guide.**
*You may reach Frances through the information below:*

One Real Estate Network
Ph. 973-714-4441

## Meet Stacey Plichta Kellar

Stacey B. Plichta ScD, CPH, is a Professor of Public Health at the City University of New York (CUNY) School of Public Health and Campus Director for the Hunter College based Bachelor's and Master's programs.

Professor Plichta has worked in academia for over 20 years teaching, advising students, and conducting her own research. Prior to coming to the CUNY School of Public Health, she was a Department Chair at Old Dominion University in Norfolk, VA. She has served on numerous academic committees, including Admissions Committees, for over 18 years. Professor Plichta has over 30 publications and has presented at numerous professional conferences. Her work focuses on how the health care system can help those who have been harmed by violence. She is married with two daughters, one who will be applying to college next year. Professor Plichta holds a doctorate in science (ScD) from the Johns Hopkins University School of Hygiene and Public Health and also completed a post-doctoral fellowship at Yale University.

*Stacey is the author of the chapter:* **Getting Yourself to College.**

## Meet Camille Re

Camille Re was a hairdresser for 10 years and then retired to stay home with her children. She is married and has four children, three girls and one boy. Two of her girls suffer from Junior Rheumatoid Arthritis and her son is diagnosed with Autism.

As a mother it was difficult for her to hold a job since she has several children with special needs. Mrs. Re's days were filled with doctor, hospital, and therapist appointments. Since she has a very necessarily busy schedule, Camille found herself looking for a home based business that allows her to have the time and freedom to take care of her work and her family. Camille is her own boss and she makes her own hours.

Camille is an Independent Distributor of an internet marketing company called Market America, Inc. Camille's title is Certified NutraMetrix Consultant. She is well versed at implementing a wellness program through advanced supplements. However she is not limited to health and wellness products. Her partners within the organization work with weight management, pet care, personal care, home and garden, auto care, internet shopping, web design, debt consolidation, cosmetics, and music. She also works as a Non-Profit Consultant. Camille loves what she does because she can offer something for everyone and help so many people with their health as well as their finances. Camille especially loves that she is able to offer a 2-35% cash back program for all of her customers.

With Market America she is a multiple Local, District, and Regional challenge winner and is a member other North Jersey Leadership Association. She now has an ongoing residual income and a business which is willable to her children.

*Camille is the author of the chapter:* **Direct Marketing: A Real Income Alternative.** *You may reach Camille through the information below:*

Camille Re
www.CRcashback.com
optimalhealth.re@gmail.com
Contact number : 862-812-0639

## Meet Arnold Rintzler

## Arnold Rintzler, Certified Business Coach

"People make the difference," says Arnie. "More than any other business variable, the development of human resources is the key to greater growth and profits."

Arnie knows his subject. He has successfully coached more than 300 individuals in 40 industries, helping them to achieve inspired leadership, employee cohesion and ultimately, greater profit. As a certified facilitator for the Total Quality Institute and Resources Associates Corporation, he has helped his clients implement "total quality management," a holistic approach to continuous business improvement.

Prior to founding AWR Business Concepts in 1993, Arnie spent 29 years in business, including 12 years as president of The Casual Woman, a chain of women's apparel stores, which he founded, grew successfully, and sold to a national retailer. He was also a senior manager for R.H. Macy Company and Federated Department Stores. He is particularly adept in buying, merchandising, operations and human resources. Arnie started AWR Business Concepts because he knows from experience that "people will willingly accomplish great things given the right support, the right tools, and the right kind of leadership."

As a business consultant, he has worked in manufacturing, construction, and retail, as well as professional and service industries. He helps clients with management issues, process improvement and strategic direction. He has facilitated the development of strategic business and marketing plans, plus leadership, sales performance and employee evaluation.

Arnie holds a degree in psychology from the University of Pittsburgh. His professional certifications include Achievement Seminars International (training and marketing), and the Resource Associate Network (affiliate and trainer). His articles have appeared in newspapers and business publications, he has been featured on radio and TV, and he has been a speaker for many business and professional groups. In addition, Arnie is an adjunct instructor at Essex County Community College and also has taught at the Community College of Morris and The Institute for Business & Professional Development at Kean University.

"Most people have a great deal of potential they're just not using," says Arnie. "We help people discover, expand and develop the skills and attitudes necessary to achieve a higher degree of success both personally and professionally."

Together we work on executing the plans we created. Often, most importantly, we generate greater cash flow that continues the growth trend.

Specialties: Trusted Advisor | Executive Coach | Entrepreneurial Consultant | Business Growth Expert | Assessment Tools | Leadership Development | Sales Development | One Page Strategic Plan.

*Arnold is the author of the chapters:* **What is Time Management?** *and*

***Goal Setting.*** *You may reach Arnold through the information below:*

Arnold@awrintzler.com
www.awrbusinessconcepts.com

## Meet Rocco Sileo

Rocco has been involved in the financial services industry for over a decade. His professional career began as a mortgage broker where he originally focused his energies on the education of homeownership benefits. After passing the NJ State Banker Exam, he was a partner in a successful mortgage company for several years before taking a serious interest in the industry of debt settlement and negotiation. In 2006, after hours of research and testing, he officially began a new business to fill the much needed void for consumers who were looking for help with their unsecured debts. Since then, Rocco served briefly on the Board at Large of T.A.S.C (The Association Of Settlement Companies); which was an industry trade group devoted to consumer awareness of best practices for debt settlement and has recently expanded his business to form a processing center on behalf of different law firms who have been retained to assist consumers negotiate debt. If you would like to speak with Rocco personally, please feel free to use the contact information below.

*Rocco is the author of the chapter:* **Debt Settlement**. *You may reach Rocco through the information below:*

Rocco Sileo
Email: rocco.legalprotection@gmail.com

## Meet
## Zoltan Simon, Esq.

Zoltan has excellent interpersonal skills, dealing with people of all backgrounds, with a proven track record. Ancillary to the practice of law, he originates residential, commercial, and reverse mortgages. He instructs the NMLS (Nationwide Mortgage Licensing System) classes for Federal Law, New Jersey Law, New York Law, and continuing education. As a Litigator in the Financial Services Industry, he has a specific skill set in state/federal regulatory compliance, including, but not limited to RESPA, TILA, HOEPA, ECOA, HMDA, SAR, KYC, Dodd Frank Act, BSA, AML, state banking laws, and FINRA for Broker/Dealer litigation.

Specialties: Litigation, Banking, Tax, Real Estate, Foreclosure, Minor Criminal, and FINRA.

- Member of the NY & CT State Bars
- Represented and Advised Brokers in regards to FINRA, NMLS, and Broker/Dealer Litigation
- NY Counsel for the National Police Defense Foundation
- New York Counsel for IPG Legal & Tax Advisors of South Korea and Kaplan Zena of Miami, FL

- Estate planning, real estate transactions and other legal and financial matters
- Negotiate Pleas, Dismissals and other Dispositions in New York Criminal Cases
- Represented investors, Lending institutions and Individuals
- Certified Guardian Ad Litem for the New York State Supreme Court
- Licensed Realtor in NY & Licensed Mortgage Loan Originator in NY, NJ, & CT

*Zoltan is the author of the chapter:* **Reverse Mortgages: A Financial Option for Seniors.** *You may reach Zoltan through the information below:*

Zoltan Simon
zoltansimonesq@gmail.com

## Meet
## Alexander Toia

Alexander Toia & Company has the resources to satisfy your investigative needs across the United States and beyond its borders. If you have any questions about how a private investigator may help you, please visit www.atoiacompany.com, or call professional Private Investigators Alex Toia or Barbara Rudd at 973-538-3338.

Alex Toia, CCLA, LPI began his private investigation career in 1973 while a graduate student at Rutgers University, School of Criminal Justice. He worked part-time as an apprentice investigator for Hamilton Detective Agency, Livingston, NJ that specialized in matrimonial surveillances and missing persons. In 1975, Alex was appointed to New Jersey's newly created Pre-Trial Intervention Program, supervised by the Morris County Probation Department and Prosecutor's Office. Background and pre-sentence investigations, defendant and witness interviews, and extensive evaluations were routinely prepared for assistant prosecutors and criminal court judges.

After three years with Morris County, before Special Investigation Units were introduced to the insurance industry, Chubb Insurance Group offered Alex a unique field investigator position to expand its Claims and Litigation Departments. For the next five years, Alex investigated all personal and commercial coverage lines, including motor vehicle claims, construction accidents, property and liability claims, personal injuries, natural and suspicious deaths, and premises liability cases. He also completed a three-year Legal Insurance course at the American Educational Institute to earn the Special Designation of Casualty Claim Law Associate (CCLA), which gives him substantial knowledge of insurance-related litigation few investigators possess.

In 1982, Alex founded Search Investigations, Inc. and specialized in insurance claims, civil litigation, and criminal defense investigations. Clients included insurance carriers, law firms, lawyers, private and public corporations, and self-insured groups throughout the New Jersey/New York Metropolitan area.

After 16 years of successful operation, Alex looked for greater, more complex challenges and merged his company with another investigative agency to form Murphy Toia Murphy, Inc. After almost five years as the company's Internal Operations Director, Alex decided to re-establish his own company where he would have full control of all internal and external operations, and could truly make a positive difference in people's lives. Hence, Alexander Toia & Company, LLC was formed.

Alex Toia has also published articles in the NALI periodical, PI Magazine, and NJLPIA.

*Alex is the author of the chapter:* **How a Private Investigator Can Help Get You Money**. *You may reach Alex through the information below:*

Alex Toia
Phone: 973-538-3338
Email: alex@atoiacompany.com.

**Meet Fern Weiss**

Parent Coach and Educator

Certified Empowerment Coach – Institute for Professional Excellence in Coaching, 2008

Certified K-12 Teacher, State of New Jersey, 2001

BA, French, Douglass College, 1977

Additional Trainings:

Social & Emotional Intelligence Coach – Institute for Social & Emotional Intelligence, 2014

Keruv Consultant for the religiously intermarried – Federation of

Jewish Men's Clubs

"The Biggest Job" © Facilitator – Hyde School program for family-based character development, 2006

Parent Coach and Educator for parents of teens and tweens. Your Family Matters, LLC

As a parent coach, former middle school teacher, and the parent of two wonderful young adults, Fern has seen all sides of parents and adolescents and the challenges they face getting through the teen years. In her work with parents, Fern shares from her personal experience as the mother of an out-of-control teen. She learned that love and good intentions were not enough… in fact, they were part of the problem. Nothing was going to change until she did. So she did, and doing that work changed everything.

Since 2008 she has been taking parents back to basics, beginning with breaking through the fears all parents have for their children that keep them worried and hovering over them.

Parents become more confident and able to do what it takes (including what feels tough) to raise self-sufficient, confident, resilient kids. Fern teaches parents to align words, decisions, values and actions to feel more in control; to stop send-guessing themselves; to hear and be heard; and to set the limits and high expectations that will prepare their children to be successful in high school, college and beyond.

*Fern is the author of the chapters:* **Who knew cleaning toilets could boost self-esteem; Are You Crippling Your Kids?; It Is Not Your Job to Make Sure Your Kids Are Happy;** *and* **College Prep***. You may reach Fern through the information below:*

www.yourfamilymatterscoach.com
fern@yourfamilymatterscoach.com
Phone: 201-747-9642

*THE END*

www.ingramcontent.com/pod-product-compliance
Lightning Source LLC
Chambersburg PA
CBHW060459090426
42735CB00011B/2043